# Rich, Handsome Exaggerator

## Howie Krakow

*"No irritation.  No pearl."*

For Debbie.

For all the right reasons.

# The end

If you're looking for a complex, highly developed plot or a surprising, tricky conclusion, you've come to the wrong book.

Here's the entire story:

1. Man looks for woman.
2. He finds her.

That's all there is to it.

This book is about a quest – an earnest search that went on for well over 20 years and in several states. It honestly took me that long to find Debbie. But the prolonged effort, as anyone who has met her will certainly attest, was well worth the time and energy.

As will hopefully become evident, even though it took more than two decades to find her, for the most part, the process was anything but painful. I certainly did my best to enjoy the peculiarities of the journey as much as possible.

I began with hopes of a happy ending. But in truth, I had no idea how happy that ending could actually be. And, although the pursuit was surely amusing, living with Debbie every day is infinitely better.

The search is over. But the happily ever after part continues.

## Timing is everything.
## Well, at least it's one thing.

We are now living in an age when emails are read hourly, texts are read instantly, and the evening news on television feels about as up to date as a monthly news magazine. Viewed in that context, this book is ancient history.

The early episodes occurred well before the turn of the century. In other words, everything happened during the same millennium when the Wright Brothers first experienced flight and people huddled around the radio listening to soap operas. Still, it was well past the era of penny postcards, nickel candy bars and most of us were no longer concerned about the poor gas mileage of our Conestoga Wagons.

Some of the encounters took place immediately before and after 9/11 - which proved to be as poor a setting for romance as it was for just about everything else. Although it's much easier to blame the Saudis, the Iraqis or George Bush for my failed romances, even if they're not solely at fault, they deserve my ire for any number of reasons anyway.

Today everyone knows someone – more likely several someones – who have coupled up after meeting online. Dating websites are a multi-million dollar industry and are now fiercely specific. There are sites for people who want to meet someone of their same religious persuasion (and they can pick from all of the major ones as well as many that have yet to emerge from cult status), someone of a specified age group (even if being a member of that group yourself constitutes wishful, youthful thinking), someone of a specific background (everything from farming to Ivy League graduates to ambidextrous chain saw jugglers) or someone whose peculiarities regarding art, education or sex line up particularly well with your own.

When I first entered the fray, the choices were slim. I think they were limited to AOL Personals, Match.com and, as far as I knew at the time, nothing else.

Of course, the fear factor loomed large. What kind of a person would be so desperate that they'd be reduced to searching cyberspace for a date, a mate or companionship? It turned out that question was one I could easily answer: me.

The "what if's" bubble to the top of a list that had never even been considered before. What if she isn't who she claims to be? What if she is older or younger than the picture she posted? How about <u>very much</u> older or younger? What if I end up writing to a guy who's only pretending to be a woman? What if I'm being lured into a den of iniquity. (OK. that wasn't really a concern and in fact would probably have been welcomed).

And what about me? What about the way I present myself in my online profile? Am I brave enough to show a current photo or will my high school graduation picture be sufficient? After all, other than the hair loss, wrinkles and glasses, I haven't changed that much in the past 30 years. How honest should I be? Should I proudly state that I am capable of not only feeding myself but also cutting up my own food? Should I mention that my name does not appear on the FBI's "Most Wanted" list (although that may be due to the fact that I have a brilliant attorney who is reputed to have a client's sodomy charges reduced to "following too closely"?

At some point, the decision to dive in overwhelmed the concerns. What's the worst that could happen? OK, the worst could actually be pretty bad but what's the second worst? So, with minimal expectations, an abundance of curiosity and a mixture of optimism and consternation I turned my MAC into a Matchmaker.

## Online dating is just like regular dating. Only different.

No matter how dating begins – meeting cute, introduced by friends or relatives, via a matchmaker, a drunken encounter between a bridesmaid and a groom at an otherwise uneventful wedding, through an online site or, in fact, any other way – the concept of dating is unique. Unlike many activities that you engage in with the goal of improving your technique, dating is something you do until you can stop. The goal is not be a proficient dater, the goal is to be an ex-dater.

On occasion, I have achieved that goal. So, if you feel an overwhelming need to work up some sympathy for me because it seems that the episodes in this book constitute my complete social activities with women during more than two decades, you can hold off a bit on your concern although even a little compassion thrown my way is always appreciated.

In truth, there were several periods when I was completely off-line – sometimes for months and occasionally even longer. The reason for my inactivity on dating sites was because I was involved in relationships. I met several women in the relatively usual way - at work or through friends. Happily – at least at first - there seemed to be reason for exclusivity. All of those relationships lasted until they didn't. They stopped for completely understandable reasons - it was entirely the woman's fault. Certainly the demise had nothing to do with my own annoying habits, disturbing peculiarities or unwillingness to commit.

The fact that I have participated in several relationships makes me somewhat of an expert on break-ups. I have heard that, on occasion, two people mutually agree to stop seeing each other and are able to separate without pain, remorse, bitterness or acrimony. Because I have never been party to such a wholesome, reasonable ending, I believe that a mutually satisfactory demise to a love affair is a figment of the imagination. As far as I'm concerned there is only one way for a break-up to occur: someone decides to become the dumper and the other person, by no choice of his or her own, becomes the dump-ee.

Both come with baggage.

Being the dumper is never easy. As a compassionate person, guilt often overwhelms. The sadness your actions cause another person – someone who has been very special to you for a significant amount of time – is a terrible burden to bear. It's almost impossible to determine how long the pain will last. Sometimes the dumper continues to suffer through an entire evening. But fortunately, by daybreak, the sun has risen and the distasteful memory slips away forever.

Being the dump-ee requires no effort at all. In a very short period of time – well, compared to an interval like, for example, the Ice Age – all is done and forgotten. In the meantime, however, there is, admittedly, some discomfort. But waking moments are easily filled with unanswerable questions and, because sleep is impossible, there is plenty of time to consider and reconsider those questions endlessly.

Friends are often available to provide comfort, help and suggestions. Their advice is remarkably similar and equally useless. Essentially what they recommend is that you get back on the horse and resume dating. It's a great idea. And one you consider seriously but end up rejecting because you:

1. are a basket case
2. incapable of even thinking about dating someone new
3. no longer have a whit of self esteem
4. barely have the energy to bathe or dress yourself
5. find it difficult to conceive of someone finding you even remotely appealing

6. are much too busy feeling sorry for yourself to consider doing anything to relieve the misery

People will tell you that you need to go out and do something to get your mind off of your sad, sad situation. They're tired of hearing you say that everything reminds you of the one who left you high and dry. Your friends will have lots of ideas. They'll almost certainly suggest taking you out to dinner. But you'll decline because "Susanne eats." (Apologies to Richard Lewis).

Food looms large for all dump-ees. For some, food becomes solace. It's the only thing that makes you feel good so you "enjoy" it often. Some might say "too often" but what do they know? They didn't just get dumped. So in the absence of a partner, you turn to what is always present: the refrigerator, take-out menus and a cabinet or two stocked with items loaded with wholesome ingredients like salt, sugar and preservatives. You've heard that chocolate is supposed to have healthful benefits and this is a great opportunity to test that theory for yourself. Because you're emotionally incapable of doing anything else, you eat. Constantly. As a bonus, that gives you something else to feel bad about.

For other dump-ees, there is an opposite reaction to food. It becomes completely inedible. All of your favorites no longer have any appeal. Your appetite is completely gone. It's not just that you don't want to eat. You simply can't. The good news is that you have now discovered what may well be the most effective weight loss program ever conceived. But before you get too impressed with your increasingly svelte body, it's a good idea to remember that when you finally emerge from this seemingly endless depression, your appetite will return and you will almost surely binge to make up for the lost calories. I have been both the dumper and the dump-ee and can state without fear of being challenged that I dislike both. But being dumped is worse. Way, way worse.

When I am ejected from a relationship, I'm totally lost. I have no energy, no sense of humor, no appetite, no desire to be with other people and take no pleasure in being by myself. I'm always tired but am unable to sleep. Other than my one activity – constantly feeling sorry for myself - I am totally useless. Curiously, even my closest friends do not find this to be particularly endearing. Perhaps if I explained my sad situation yet again, they might change their minds.

Fortunately, like everything else, this feeling of loss, desperation, sadness, inadequacy and despondency is only a phase. It too shall pass. In a few weeks, a few months, a year or two at the very most, all this pain will be history. In the meantime however, it sucks the big one. Every single minute of every single day.

If you've ever been there, you know exactly what I'm talking about. You know there's not a whit of exaggeration about the overwhelming, constant feeling of sadness and helplessness encompassed in a shroud of darkness that colors your every waking moment. And if you've never been dumped on and never felt any of that excruciating, endless pain, do the rest of us a favor and go fuck yourself.

## Great Expectations.
## Mediocre Expectations.
## No Expectations at all.

In many ways, even in the very early days of online dating sites, my reason to participate was not very complicated.

Just as I would happily be willing to meet a woman recommended by a trusted friend, the prospect of meeting someone who I had only gotten to know via email correspondence seemed like a reasonable thing to do.

The expectations weren't very different. And frankly, I had no idea what to expect. I didn't know how the process worked. I didn't know the rules. I didn't even know if there <u>were</u> rules.

But once I made the decision to participate, I felt comfortable knowing that I'd be able to decide relatively quickly whether I'd want to continue.

It wasn't a major commitment. The cost was minimal. And I knew I'd have complete control over the communication. No one was going to make me meet someone I had no interest in meeting.

Did I think this was the route to meeting the woman I'd want to spend the rest of my life with? While that would have been nice, it was hardly a consideration. I'd be happy just finding someone to spend an enjoyable evening with. Anything more than that would be a bonus.

As it turned out, I got to spend enjoyable evenings with several women I never actually met. Exchanging emails with strangers definitely has its upside. It's a peculiar combination of real communication and total anonymity. The unanticipated benefit is that you can say whatever you want and the only restrictions are the ones you put on yourself. Occasionally, there is mutual reason to get together for something innocuous like a cup of coffee. But even more frequently there is no reason to go beyond the emails. And you don't have to provide a reason for stopping the communication. You just don't respond any more. Or, what is more likely, you don't receive any more emails.

Rejection – especially when it happens in person – almost can't help being hurtful. But being rejected by someone you haven't met isn't troublesome at all. If you don't actually know them, who cares if they don't want to know you? You simply move on because, as it turns out, there are lots and lots of unexpected options.

True, there are many frogs. But you don't have to kiss them and you don't even have to meet them. The good news is that there is almost certainly to be someone who piques your interest and who, for reasons that need not be quantified, is interested in communicating with you as well.

What happens after that is up to the two of you... just like real life. Odds are that this may not be your match of a lifetime. But if you're playing the odds, this is definitely a way to increase the possibilities.

I was unquestionably lucky when I met Debbie. I was also persistent. And unwilling to settle for a runner-up.

The also-rans were what kept things interesting along the way. The path was seldom straight and not without its bumps and bruises. But that's what made the final chapter so worthy of the effort.

As the saying goes..."no irritation, no pearl".

# A Brief History of Online Hook Ups in the late 20th Century

Yes, Virginia, dating actually did pre-date computers.

Today (this being a day in the year 2019) online dating is well accepted to the point of being commonplace. But way back in the pre-historic days (before smart phones, computers and electric cars) such a concept was considered suspicious - if only due to the scarcity of anything even remotely cyber-ish.

Until recently, those who wished to find romance, companionship and, especially lifetime mates, had limited resources. They got acquainted at work, school, church, community meetings, or anyplace where they happened to bump into each other (an activity Hollywood termed as "meeting cute." There were, of course, any number of brothers, sisters, aunts and a whole host of friends who, miserable in their own relationships, felt compelled to encourage others to join their pity party.

Meeting in bars was specifically frowned upon for varied and nefarious reasons. Among them: noise at decibel levels that made meaningful conversation difficult, the spurious quality of people who frequented establishments serving alcoholic beverages (oneself not included of course) and most of all, impaired judgment caused by over indulgence that was followed immediately by the misguided, but ultimately correct realization, that everyone's visual attributes improve considerably as closing time approaches.

Matchmaking on a professional, semi-pro or amateur level has been around since the moment Adam and Eve got fixed up. So it's hardly surprising that with a well-established desire for connection but without a proven method of creating meaningful introductions in the modern era, it fell upon resourceful minds to invent a solution. Avarice, as is often the case, came to the rescue.

In short order, the route to true romance was not paved by romantics but by those who envisioned a way to monetize love. Entrepreneurs fervently chasing the almighty buck uncovered a brilliant opportunity in the classified section of daily newspapers. "Personals" were born and it appeared that the Fifth Estate had invented yet another means of maintaining life support.

Almost immediately, classified sections of newspapers and, soon afterwards, magazines too, expanded as hopefuls of every age began looking for lifelong companions or even a less permanent romantic interlude via this new resource.

For a while – actually quite a while – the possibilities of true love bloomed, the print medium thrived and all was well with the world. But, as all good things eventually evolve, with the arrival of the internet, everything changed. Ubiquitous computers made it even easier for lonely hearts to exchange photographs and express their desire to share moonlit beach walks, cozy evenings by the fire and other indulgences that seldom occur in real life. They also discovered seemingly endless ways of stretching the truth about their own physical and financial attributes - pretty much in real time and at quite reasonable prices.

For the love-seekers, it was a boon. But for print media, not so much. Truth be told, along with the internet's greater potential for magical matches there came – almost simultaneously - the inevitable demise of magazines and newspapers Personals.

I, willingly, happily and enthusiastically, participated in every bit of the evolution. I responded to personal ads in New York magazine, partook of the early opportunities available in free online exchanges and eventually joined some of the more fleshed out internet services that were heavily promoted on television.

With almost no misgivings and a paucity of angst, I threw myself into the breach. My reasoning was simple: at worst, I'd emerge with at least a few stories worth telling and, at best, the love of my life.

As it turns out, I got both.

# Slaughtering Lambs

There was a lull in the action.

To be more accurate, it was something longer than a lull. There was certainly no equivocating about the lack. Quite simply, in terms of action, there was none.

All of the known routes had been well traveled. Fix-ups from friends had dwindled to nothing, there was no one I knew casually that I wanted to know better, checking the Personals section of the classified ads revealed more information about massages and escort services than I wanted to know and internet dating was still years away from its infancy.

Because I was at pretty much of a loss, I proceeded under the theory that doing something would be better than not doing anything.

It is, after all, a reasonable theory. Occasionally, it even works. And for me, staying home and calling no one had already shown predictable results. Status remained quo.

So I reasoned that taking a shot – even if the possibility of success was remote – at least offered an outside chance for success. While the fantasy of being rewarded with the woman of my dreams may have been close to non-existent, there was, nevertheless, always the potential of at least coming away with a decent story.

Decent or not, this is the story:

Although I don't remember precisely how I received it, I accepted an invitation to attend what I have been referring to as a Lamb Slaughtering Party. I suspect that the organizing group and its membership use a more complimentary name but I stand by my choice. It may not be completely accurate but it's definitely in the right direction.

While other groups may have been assembled for the sole purpose of cornering potential Sugar Daddies, my personal experience is only with this one. Here's how it works:

It begins with a loose amalgam of women – although definitely not an amalgam of loose women. All are considerably over the age of 40 and all, for one reason or another, are relentlessly engaged in the pursuit of a suitable man. In some cases, they are widows. In some cases they are divorced. In some cases they have simply looked at their own visions in the mirror and noticed a distinct and disturbing length of tooth. Realizing that they share a common goal, they have banded together *to do something about it.*

In addition to any number of other methods they might also employ, in this particular instance they have combined efforts, pooled a bit of mutual money, and done their level best to assemble a list of suitably available male prospects.

The list is constantly revised and added to. Notes on all potential male attendees are rigorously kept. Those who pass muster are invited to carefully planned events and encouraged - almost to the point of annoyance – to bring along with them other suitable, unattached male companions of a certain financial status. Further qualifications seem to be limited to the ability to stand with or without a supporting device and a willingness to sign checks that include a sufficient number of commas before the decimal point.

Arrangements are carefully made for a cocktail party. The timing, as well as its location, is of considerable import.

Location first. Usually, a member of the group offers her own apartment. Invariably it is located in Manhattan – often in a relatively prestigious building. Many of the women are already affluent, either from former marriages, the luck of a silver-spooned birth or, quite possibly, due to their own efforts. The location says a lot about the group. It says "This is not a party of wanabees. We are women who are doing quite well, thank you very much." While that may be somewhat of an exaggeration for all of the women who participate, certainly the hostess with the hoity-toity apartment is not overly concerned about where her next hot meal is coming from.

Timing too, has been well thought-out and adhered to with almost militaristic precision. The event lasts exactly 2 hours – from 6 until 8 p.m. In New York, that may seem to be curiously early. But there is no mistake here. As it is with many other worthwhile endeavors, timing is everything.

Even though limited hors d'oeuvres are served, the proffered tidbits are hardly a substitute for a proper meal. And therein lies the brilliance. With some luck and, more likely, considerable effort, each woman's goal is to find herself in deep, meaningful conversation with one of the guests. Faced by the frustration of the party's non-retractable cut-off time, she suggests that the fascinating verbal exchange be continued – say, over dinner. Because the gentleman has obviously committed to the evening's event, odds are at least fairly good that he has no other plans for the rest of the night. And, by happy coincidence, the woman is also available. How fortunate.

Amazingly, even though there are several dozen women in attendance, none of them have dinner plans. Is that a lucky happenstance or what?

The guest list has been culled, worked on and worked over for quite some time. All of the women submit names and provide as much description as possible. This is not an assignment taken lightly. Invariably, the criteria are considerable. All invited men need to be relationship

21

material. That means they need to be available, financially successful, and of appropriate age. Of these categories, "available" is important" "financially successful" is crucial and " age appropriate" covers a wide and forgiving swath. Visual appearance, while it could be a plus, is a non-factor. Slothfulness is not appreciated but nevertheless tolerated. It is a given that all invitees will be of sufficient height when standing on their checkbooks.

"Available" means not currently in a relationship. Divorced is best and separated is OK. Never married is not a great indicator of potential success, but depending on the number of men who have accepted invitations and the desperation quotient of the women, sometimes even confirmed bachelors have been known to survive the cut.

"Successful" means more than simply being employed. These women don't want a guy with a job. They're not looking for blue collar, minimum wage material. Some of them already have their own money – and plenty of it. What they'd really like is a guy who looks good in a suit, holds some sort of executive or professional position and who will be an appropriate arm piece. They will, however, happily settle for someone with a bucket load of blue chip stocks and a willingness to support them in the style to which they would like to become accustomed. It is not considered a deal breaker if the man in question has a monogrammed walker and only occasionally drools on his finely pressed, Egyptian combed cotton shirt.

Age is not a criterion because these women are realists. They'd be thrilled to be with a younger guy, but realize that, for most of them, the time for youthful companionship has long since passed. So almost all of the men in attendance are a few years pre - or several years post - retirement. Perhaps a smattering are younger than 60. But many are likely to see 70 only in their rear view mirror.

There is a deliberate exclusive feeling to the affair. Invitations to the event are printed and sent via stamped, snail mail. RSVP's are not only encouraged but are vigorously and relentlessly pursued. If need be, there are follow-up phone calls. This is no hit or miss operation. These are smart, committed women who are highly focused on their mission.

The food, albeit intentionally limited, is well presented. However it doesn't take very long for the table to be strewn with half-eaten celery sticks, crumbled cheese and broken crackers. The drinks are simple – wine, soft drinks and water. Crystal and fine china has been eschewed in favor of plastic everything. The women know from experience that old men with shaky hands are prone to the occasional case of dropsies and that red wine is always the first to be spilled.

These well-planned events happen on a somewhat regular basis. So it would be reasonable to assume that the participating women who go to such great effort to plan and execute them consider their time and energy well spent.

But for me, that was not the case. And it didn't take long to come to that realization.

Clearing the first hurdle – getting past the building's doorman – was easy. I had my invitation; he had a guest list and his orders. So far, so good.

As soon as I exit the elevator, a woman seated at a reception table in the hallway cheerfully greets and welcomes me. Her job is to monitor the guest list and make certain that members of the Great Unwashed are kept away. Although I pass muster because my name matches precisely one on her roster, until I eventually make my exit later in the evening, this is the last time I'll feel even remotely comfortable

From the moment I enter the apartment's front door, I am immediately ill at ease. There is good reason.

I know no one – not a single man and not a single woman. It is still a mystery as to how or why I was invited. In addition, I stand out like the guy who farted in the elevator. Of all men in attendance, I am the only one who is not wearing a suit and tie. Either they have all come directly from work or they are the kind of men who, in retirement, continue to dress as if they have daily meetings with bankers and fellow board members. Not a single one of them has so much as removed a jacket or loosened a tie – a condition that will remain unchanged for the duration of the party.

I, too, have come directly from work. But my office attire is somewhat different. I'm wearing jeans and a Hawaiian shirt. For me, this is dress up clothes. Anytime I'm sporting leather shoes and a shirt that doesn't have either writing or someone else's name on it, I'm feeling pretty damned slick. Even though that may not be apparent to others, my wardrobe is as fancy/dancy as I'm likely to get.

From the first moment on, I spend the evening hiding in plain sight. Surprisingly, my intensely brightly colored shirt does not make me a target. It does precisely the opposite because the kind of guy these women are after doesn't do casual. To them, I couldn't be more invisible if I was dressed like the dining room wallpaper and stood motionless next to the breakfront.

The men are attired in suits that cover the entire color spectrum from gray to dark blue. But the women have definitely dressed for the occasion. Even those who have come directly from the office are no longer in office clothes. They are on the prowl and are suitably attired for the hunt.

Not surprisingly, they avoid me as if I'm wearing work out clothes with sweat stained armpits. Although I feel totally out of place, there is a reason why I am not entirely unhappy about being ignored.

Frankly, these women scare me.

There is not a smile in the lot. The conversations I overhear are banal, boring and repetitive. I know - not because I'm involved in any of them - but because I'm an excellent eavesdropper. It's a personal hobby. Often I hear gems – tidbits of phrases that are hysterical, unusual, or delightfully incomprehensible. I savor the words and often incorporate them in my writing.

But at this party, I hear little worth remembering. Is it possible that everyone here is dull and humorless? Of course, my own discomfort unquestionably colors my judgment, but apparently, against all odds this group has taken boring to new lows.

It's not surprising that no one wants to talk to me. To them, I'm the hunchbacked intruder. But I am surprised that there is no one that I want to talk to either. It's true that I'm too intimidated to strike up a conversation but as I survey the room, there is no one whose story I would like to know better – or even at all. My eavesdropping skills have revealed a depressing truth: underneath those gray suits are equally gray personalities.

The men all seem to be caricatures. A few stand erect but many hunch over, tightly gripping their plastic glasses of wine as they hover around the food table. Some load up a plate, spilling less than half of the items selected. Men of a certain age are undeniably clumsy. That's not an unfair generalization. It's a fact. Crumbs stick to their faces; wine spills on their shirts and still tightly knotted ties. But they never notice. Never.

It's not clear whether or not the men are in on the gag. They huddle in front of the meager food table as if it was a

25

resplendent buffet. They return for more wine and fill their plastic glasses so close to the brim that spills are assured. They seem oblivious to the fact that they're at a hunting party and that they are the ones being hunted.

The women, on the other hand, do not hesitate. They have arrived in full attack mode. I watch them scan the room and isolate their prey. Invariably the guy with the most expensive, best fitting suit draws first blood. But, even though he is capable of chewing, he seems unable to grunt through his share of the conversation. No matter. The Armani suit is more than sufficient. Once cornered, he remains pinned in position. For a while I observe this lamb being prepared for slaughter but soon it becomes too painful. I circulate.

Gloom both follows and precedes me. Somehow – almost magically - the day-glo colors and gaudy flowers on my shirt continue to make me invisible. In a room of gray and navy blue suits, I am camouflaged - a stealth bachelor working his way to the drink table, completely hidden, totally under the radar.

By now I have been here for 20 minutes - a half hour at the most. It feels much longer because every moment has been painfully awkward. There has not been a second when I am not positive that I don't belong here. I know that the discomfort is all self generated. I'm the only one who knows that I'm a fish out of water – no one else even realizes that I'm here. No one will know if I leave. My absence, just like my presence, is a non-factor.

I am now faced with two choices: 1. Refill my plastic cup with sparkling water that no longer sparkles and continue to observe the painful drama that surrounds me, or 2. Make my getaway. It's a non- decision: I choose option #2 and serpentine towards the door.

It is unsurprising that no one intentionally impedes my progress or falls prostrate before me in an effort to convince me to stay.

My goodbyes are severely limited because I have no idea who the hostess is, whose apartment I'm in, or who to thank for the lovely plastic cup, the fizz-less water or the pageant that I have witnessed, albeit not participated in.

As I ease door-ward, I observe another important ritual in progress. One certain way to encourage the making of dinner arrangements is to cut off the supply of food and drink. It's the equivalent of blinking the lights to announce last call.

Two women begin – very obviously - to clear the table as I make my way to the door. Although the party is still in full swing, the women want to make sure that the men understand that it's close to closing time. But, even as the last tidbits of food are unceremoniously swept away, as long as a few pretzels and chips remain, the elderly gentlemen continue to munch. They may be rich, but free food is free food.

Seemingly unfazed by the poor table manners, the women continue to stalk. For a moment I think I hear some actual conversation and, is it possible, some laughter as well?

Sadly, I will never know. I shut it quietly but firmly behind me. Then I exhale.

In some ways, after I exit the elevator, pass through the lobby and find myself outdoors, I feel as if I have escaped. My mission was accomplished. Even though I didn't interact with a single person, at least I got a story - perhaps not a particularly good one, but a story nevertheless.

Two weeks later I receive a phone call inviting me to another of these get-togethers. I'm also asked, "in the spirit of nice people knowing other nice people" if I know someone – specifically some other man - who might like to attend a future event".

In a rash, compulsive act of abject honesty, I explain that I know no other bachelors (a relatively true statement) and that I, myself, felt uncomfortable at the last event and can't envision myself returning. Because I am now cruising on a roll of sincerity, I add that I will not be grief stricken if I am permanently stricken from their list of prey.

This momentous news is hardly received with anguish. And, despite the admirable attempt at expressing sorrow, it's clear that I will not be missed. Even over the phone, I think I can almost hear the pen drawing a thick black line through my name.

# My Prequel to Internet Dating

As a long-standing, cover-to-cover reader of New York Magazine, I began to notice the Personals section in the back of the book. With no purpose and no reason save my own entertainment, I began to read a few. Eventually, I started reading *all* of them. That was no minor commitment because, as the weeks progressed, so did the size of the Personals section. What had begun as a half column of small type ads soon morphed into page upon page of "Men Seeking Women", "Women Seeking Men" and a seemingly unlimited combination of "Whoever Seeking Whatever".

The thought of actually becoming a participant took a long time to develop. But, as I read more ads – including several that actually piqued my interest – the concept of responding began to creep into my consciousness.

The risk seemed minimal. And the potential benefit of meeting someone I would never encounter any other way started to have increasing appeal.

So, with the arrival of each weekly issue of New York magazine, I read the postings with greater care and, on occasion, mentally marked a few that might – just possibly might – warrant a note from me.

Eventually I succumbed. I held my breath, closed my eyes and jumped in. Because decades have elapsed since that initial venture, I have at best a fuzzy memory of what happened. I know I wrote only a handful of responses that, in turn, led to very few actual face-to-face meetings. Some of those meetings were easily forgettable (as evidenced by the fact that I don't remember anything about them) and others, while of slightly greater consequence, never led to more than a single meeting.

I didn't save any of the Personals that I responded to. With a lone exception, I didn't save any of the correspondence.

It's quite possible that little was written and the only communication occurred by phone. I kept no notes about any of the women I met. I don't recall what we did, where we met or what was talked about. While all of that is certainly missing, I doubt that anyone – including me - is inconsolable over the tragic loss.

One of the few (actually the only) remnants is this letter I sent to a woman whose posting, in addition to generating interest for other reasons, requested that potential suitors write her a poem.

To the poetry-seeker, along with the letter (which was printed and sent by regular snail mail to a New York Magazine P.O. Box) I included a photo of James Garner and myself that was taken during a TV commercial production. The thought being that even if she found me uninteresting at least she might be impressed by my proximity to an A-lister.

As I re-read the note, it's pretty evident that the process of writing to her definitely amused me. Based on her lack of response, that amusement was clearly not reciprocated.

Dear 8117,

A poem?

Problem is, I think you're serious. In a funny way, of course. But your request seems genuine, nonetheless.

Well, verse, I can do. Ogden Nash, Shel Silverstein, sure. Maybe I could even toss a dirty limerick your way. But somehow I get the feeling that ain't gonna cut it.

You want real poetry, right? Deep and meaningful. Symbolic and powerful. Touched with alliteration and perhaps even a bit of rhyme (although probably not too much – blank verse currently being considered either the most sophisticated or at least the most pretentious).

And what for a subject? There's doom and gloom aplenty in the headlines these days. But those stories seem better suited to sound bites than couplets. Here's another thought: it is springtime and it must have been seconds at least since the words "moon, June and bloom" have been linked. No, that's a pass, too.

How about love? Plenty of fresh new, territory there. How could I miss? After all, the competition is limited to – oh, let's be conservative – maybe just the 127 greatest poets of all time.

So, whaddya want: truth, beauty, pathos, depth, insight, pith, vision ... or would you settle for a chuckle?

Does it have to be an original poem? What if I just copied some obscure verses but, in my desire to impress, somehow neglected to give credit where credit was due? For example, do you know the one that begins, "She walks in beauty...?" OK, I was just asking.

31

Are you beginning to get the feeling that your poem is not going to be included in this letter? That I'm just procrastinating? That perhaps poetry is not my strong suit?

Not necessarily true. There's a lot of latitude given to contemporary poetry. It's all in the way that the words are read. Or, at the very least, in the way that they're typed.

For example:

What if I wrote a paragraph
this way?
Thereby providing significance to the words
on each line... even if there was only one word
on a given
line.
Would that be a poem?
Or would it still just be lousy writing
made even worse
by ridiculous construction?

You don't have to answer - that was a rhetorical question. And about as close to writing or receiving a poem as either of us is likely to come at this time.

But, other than that, I have to admit that I read your ad several times and was unable to find the fatal flaw. It's not that I'm on a determined quest for imperfection - it's just that I've learned that what appears to be too good to be true, quite often turns out, in fact, to be too good to be true.

Nevertheless, it might be fun trying to discover the disconnect. After all, what's not to like about brainy, beautiful and fit? The same certainly holds true for creative, sweet, sophisticated and sexy.

And, yet your desires are so minimal; so easily satisfied. Is it possible that all you request in a man is "someone who is successful, open to life and ready for love"? (Does the fact that I gave so freely of myself to save France not matter at all?)

Fully realizing the enormous risk of injury that might incur while patting myself on the back, I'd like to think that I measure up to your pretty daunting standards. But since, at this point, we're dealing primarily in self-evaluation, I would venture that most men judge themselves to be qualifiers. However, if you've already followed up on any responses to your ad, my guess is that your own definition may be somewhat at odds with the men who presented themselves as candidates.

The enclosed photo provides, at the very least, evidence of my existence. Just a helpful note - I'm the one who isn't the movie star. But, you have to admit, I am wearing a sillier shirt.

This is what I looked like 3 months ago. (Frankly, I haven't aged much since then). Other pertinent information: I'm the divorced father of 2 sons in their early 20's. I lived in LA for nearly 20 years where I wrote TV and film with a fair amount of financial success, but very little personal satisfaction.

So, about 6 years ago, I chose the artistic high road and moved east to pursue a career where morality, integrity and ethics would be appreciated and respected. Fortunately, when the plane landed, I came to my senses. I am now a partner at an advertising agency that is among the largest and most successful in New York.

Details, infinitely more personal information, and, who knows, maybe even a spirited discussion of poetry will happily be furnished upon request. Over coffee. Or dinner. Or the phone.
Your choice.

Howie 000-000-000


**Note:**

Apparently Miss 8117 did not appreciate my attempt at humor, my inability to supply a poem, the photo of James Garner or anything else that I had to offer. I, however, enjoyed myself thoroughly.

# Friday Night at the Lonely Hearts Club

The initial foray into the world of internet dating begins with optimism and innocence. It is assumed, although quite inaccurately, that the other participants, like you, have no ulterior motives.

It doesn't take long, however, for reality to set in. There are many players who seem to have much more on their minds than a satisfactory conclusion to a search for a lifetime mate. Where some see romance and blissful coupledom, others see business opportunity.

This is a story about a pitiful attempt to use the internet to generate some income. As is often the case, it begins with a semblance of hope and ends with at least a modicum of disappointment.

But I'm getting ahead of myself. Fair warning, though: a "happily ever after" conclusion should not be anticipated. Fortunately, however, there will be attempted amusement in the interim.

The story starts here with an email from Nicky.

*What a pleasure to read your profile... and your face ain't bad either. I am having a very small soiree in my home this Friday nite and I would love to see you there. Highly intelligent, professional men and women over 40. I would have wanted to keep you all to myself, but alas and alack...mostly a lack of the qualifications you asked for I personally cannot supply. I'm under schoolgirl230. Please call me if you can make it on Friday. 000-000-0000.*

*Nicky*

Hi Nicky -

What qualifications do you lack? I didn't specify much. The requisites included smart and funny and not much else. Clearly those are hurdles that you cleared with ease.

About Friday night...unfortunately I already have plans. There is always, of course, the possibility of changing them. You wanna entice me further or at least make me feel terrible that I can't make it?

Howie


*Hi Howie*

*Far be it for me to cajole you into coming to a perfectly lovely, interesting, spirited and comfortable cozy soiree. Anyhow I try not to tell people to change plans because I don't like it done to me, as much as I would like to meet with you. I guess you didn't look up my profile or else you would have understood our mismatch or mishmosh..Im older and taller than you. But if you play scrabble you needn't stand up and we can talk and talk and talk. Also if you want to IMail me at 9;00 tonite that would be fun. Im slow and a people person to boot. This machine intimidates me. It also cheats at scrabble.*

*Nicky*

Hi Nicky -

Tonight AOL did everything but crash. Apparently it decided that I shouldn't be sending or receiving emails.

The fact that you got mine - in spite of their clear declaration that it wasn't sent - is pretty amazing.
I'm fine at typing on this machine, but encouraging it to sit up and do tricks is beyond my capacity. Amazingly, however, I was actually able to look you up online - and I was so pleased with myself, I had to spend about a half hour of back patting for the accomplishment. I now understand that you are, as indicated, older and taller. But you look great, and that has to count for something.

Nevertheless, I think I'm going to stay with my plans. It feels like the right thing to do in spite of your very tempting offer.

My Scrabble game is not particularly good. I have friends who simply dazzle whilst I plod forever trying to think of ways to use more than 4 tiles. This is the game that separates the crossword puzzle people from the rest of us.

Have a great evening on Friday.

Howie

**At this point there is a bonus email from me**

Nicky -

Just got a call from my Friday Night Plans. My friend is going to LA for some meetings and won't return until Sunday morning. So, let's talk some more about the soiree if the invitation is still open.

Howie

Now the Story Unfolds ...

When Nicky and I began our email exchange I was barely into my first week of the on-line dating experience and hadn't yet met anyone in person. I didn't realize that our goals were not actually aligned. I was looking for a match. Nicky was looking for a paying client.

Nicky claimed to be a therapist. Although I never saw her diploma I have no trouble believing that she had a degree. My own therapist aside, I've not met any who aren't completely nuts. I think it's a requirement. If you can pass a sanity test, you're out.

After our brief email exchanges, she and I spoke on the phone a few times. She had a wealth of interesting information – all of it about herself. A torrid love affair had just ended and she was seeking solace.

Who better to confide in than me? True, we had never met and didn't know each other at all, but is that any reason not to provide personal, emotional and uncomfortable sexual stories in great detail?

I think there was one basic reason why she was willing to open herself up to me: everyone else she knew was already tired of hearing each and every aspect of her story multiple times and in laborious detail.

Frankly, I only heard it once, and I was tired of it, too. As a special favor, I'll omit the specifics. It's not because I'm discrete or capable of keeping a secret. It's just that it's a story that's been told too many times before.

Essentially the guy wanted out. So he left. That's pretty much it.

But, as is always the case with the one left behind, there is endless analysis: what happened, what didn't happen, and what should have happened.

Of course, the only issue that really matters is what will happen. And, in this case - as well as so many others - the answer is: nothing.
The guy ain't comin' back. No how. No time. No way.

The bloom is off the rose. This flower is dead. Even though it may be dried, pressed and cherished forever, it's still dead.

We spoke about this death on two occasions. Each call lasted close to an hour. Surprisingly, at the end of the call, the romance was still over and Nicky was still unhappy about that.

It is perhaps more astonishing that even with all of my vast knowledge and non-stop success in relationships, I was unable to help.

Not until she re-told every episode of her sad story was Nicky able to move on to other subjects. Eventually she told me about her Friday night get-togethers. She referred to them soirees. After attending one, I would call them something else: a way for Nicky to earn extra money without leaving home.

On Friday nights Nicky does her best to assemble about a dozen men and women at her apartment in Brooklyn Heights. Ostensibly the purpose is for them to meet each other and hopefully find someone they'd like to know better. But to be completely accurate, it's nothing more than a way Nicky has devised to help cover her rent.

Each event is an informal gathering that lasts about 2 hours. Nicky supplies the refreshments (a very generous word to describe the meager glop of processed cheese, tiny plate of broken crackers and limited selection of soft drinks and water). She also provides a few uncomfortable chairs and a slightly less than acceptable amount of air conditioning.

The guests supply themselves, some strained conversation, and $25 apiece (payable in cash immediately upon arrival). Nicky, because of her vast professional experience, has given herself the title of "facilitator". It is unclear precisely what it is that she facilities but undoubtedly she could provide an explanation. You might reasonably ask what happens at these Friday night soirees that makes them worth $25. Because the question is unanswerable, let's simply stay confined to what actually occurs.

Nicky offers a brief welcome and explains the purpose of the get-together. It's a somewhat unnecessary kick-off because it becomes immediately apparent that I am the only person who is new to the group. Everyone else has heard this set up before. Which begs another unanswerable question: why are they willing to pony up $25 to hear it again?

The gist of Nicky's introduction is that we are all wonderful, bright, exciting, attractive and consummately interesting people. Let's learn more about each other, shall we?

What ensues is an enlightening 'round the room presentation of personal, verbal resumes. Of the 2 hours we will uncomfortably spend together, about an hour and a half is expended by people who already know each other (save me, of course) re-telling who they are, what they're looking for in a mate and what makes them worthy of being half of a wonderful couple.

I am the only man who is not wearing a suit. This, in spite of the fact, that the temperature during the day has been well into the 90's and even now, at 7 p.m., despite the pathetic efforts of Nicky's air conditioner that rumbles and trembles in the window, the heat might still be reasonably described as "unbearable." Nevertheless, the men wear their suits, their ties and their jackets. I think at one point, with perspiration dripping down both sides of his face, one of them men loosens his tie. But maybe I was just hallucinating. Extreme heat does strange things to the mind.

What is even worse than the heat is what happens: everyone speaks. It's hard to remember precisely what they say. Most of them talk in monotones and with the same level of interest and enthusiasm that college professors use when describing some arcane and entirely insignificant occurrence. The only difference is that with the college professor you know you may be tested so you occasionally make a heroic, albeit often futile attempt, at listening.

Here, there is no such motivation.

When these folks speak, eyelids droop. They have nothing to say but go to extreme effort to say it poorly. And slowly. Boor #1 has been married twice and divorced an equal number of times. The divorces are easily understood; how he convinced someone to marry him in the first place will forever remain a mystery.

He speaks softly, painstakingly and in a continuous drone. Thirty seconds into his 10 minute self soliloquy, I'm fighting to stay awake. It's a battle in which I will continue to engage for the duration of the evening.

This guy has a truly unique way of explaining his buoyant philosophy. He offers us a brilliant visual interpretation to help us understand. It is one well worth remembering. With considerable pride, he tells us, "I'm the kind of guy who views the glass as half full."

I think he's off by about half. This is a guy who views the glass as Always Empty. Dried, wiped clean, turned upside down and stored in a cabinet with the doors closed and locked securely.

I know he said more. God knows he continued to talk. He must have used words and I'm pretty sure that he spoke in English. But I can't help with content. I don't have a clue. Mercifully, sometime before the entire room completely zoned out, he stopped.

One of Nicky's responsibilities as facilitator is to probe for more information. She does that later on with some of the other people – especially those who seem to need help forming complete sentences. But with this guy, Nicky is as paralyzed as the rest of us.

Her response to him is, "Thank you. Next."

Next is a woman. Her story is completely different. She offers essentially the same information that all the other women will parrot: her life couldn't possibly be better. She's active, interested, continually busy, and having the best time of her life. She has escaped a bad marriage – but left without vindictiveness. She felt terrible that she had to ask the bloke to get out of her life, but she knew there was no other choice. Obviously her ex is miserable without her. She does feel a pang of conscience about abandoning the poor sap that she carried for so long. But, surely this is for the best. Just look at how wonderfully her life has progressed since the split.

Frankly, I'm mystified by the enthusiasm of the women. According to them, their lives are so fulfilling, so happy, so richly rewarding ... where is there even a sliver of space for someone to participate in it with them?

I never ask that question. I really don't care. But it does seem peculiar that all of the women have taken the same course in positive expression. I assume they are operating under the theory that the best way to attract men is by making them feel unneeded and unnecessary.

One of the women is an artist. By fortunate coincidence she just so happens to have her portfolio with her. It's in a convenient, easy-to-carry case the size of a dining room table. In addition she has thoughtfully brought along a few samples of her textile work.

She recently completed a series that, by her own admission and quite to her amazement, has never been done before. With great pride and a hint of false modesty she unveils her breakthrough and explains her accomplishment.

She has taken large pieces of silk – about 4 feet square – and painted images of the Holocaust on them. As she explains it, her creations are not only works of art; they are also practical. She has invented a totally new accessory. She calls them "scarves". With understandable pride, she passes them around.

Why yes, a close look does reveal the subtle references to death and interminable suffering. Look, there's a swastika, here are people screaming in anguish, and there – who would have guessed - are smokestacks spewing grisly fumes. Well, won't this make a wonderful conversation starter?  And, best of all, it accessorizes with just about anything – especially in New York's favorite color – black.

She, along with the rest of us, is astounded to find that for unaccountable reasons, these silk masterpieces are not selling. Really. The fashion industry is just so damned fickle.

One of the men is a non-stop jokester. He is fast with his quips, constantly offering hysterical puns that serve as a running commentary while the personal stories unfold. For some reason, the rest of us aren't quite as adept at understanding his humorous references. Each clever barb is met with deadly silence. But he has a solution. He condescendingly explains his jokes, and as he does, he can't help chuckling at his rapier wit.

One of the women has failed to take the "my life is perfect" course. Instead, she has graduated from the school of "I'm too nervous to even say my own name out loud." We don't learn a great deal about her even though Nicky tries to draw her out with brilliantly conceived comments and questions like, "That's a beautiful dress. Where did you get it?

Her answer, "I don't remember" is not especially helpful. But then, it's not such a tragedy either. Just between us, the question was only a ploy – the dress really isn't that attractive.

Another of the men tells us why he is looking for someone to share his life. Apparently his marriage hadn't been a happy one and it was all his wife's fault. She was, "stupid, an ignoramus, she never read a book in her life, an idiot, a dumbbell, incapable of carrying on an intelligent conversation, and a pain in the ass." That may not have been an exact quote – but it certainly conveys the gist of his feelings about the woman who shared his life for 20 years.

What is truly amazing is that no matter how many terrible things he says about his ex-wife, none of those comments seemed to make him more appealing. In fact, some people seem to regard him as a bit of an overbearing jerk. Imagine that.

After the introductions, we still have about a half hour left for deep, thoughtful conversation and witty repartee. Unfortunately, despite my enormous interest in every word that was spoken, the important topics discussed, the depth of knowledge that was plumbed and the almost scandalous demonstration of wit, everything that transpired escapes me now.

Actually, the word "escape" is quite appropriate. It was the only thought that crossed my mind all evening long as I tried to determine the earliest moment when I could reasonably make my exit. Happily it came even before the 2 hours allocated for the soiree had completely elapsed. One of the women needed to leave early. I followed her so closely that if she had stopped suddenly, I could have been charged with deviant sexual behavior.

Despite Nicky's offer that the conversation could continue at a local coffee shop, the rest of the gathering also crept to its collective feet and edged towards the door. Apparently the woman who is leaving early had arranged for a car service so anyone who joined her could get a free ride and save the $1.50 subway fare. Obviously, even for the big spenders who populated the group, that was too enticing an offer to pass up. In moments, the room emptied.

In many ways, I felt sorry for everyone. To me, their lives seemed pretty lonely; pretty empty. And, based on what they had offered during the previous hours, there seemed little hope for change.

Although my own prospects had not improved one iota as a result of the evening, I was still pleased that I made the effort.

After all, I didn't come away completely empty-handed.

At least, I got a story.

# Successful Failure

My personal experience during a long, relatively sustained period of being fixed up, attending singles events, responding to classified ads in the Personals sections of magazines and participating in some online dating sites was, almost to a woman, surprisingly positive.

That hardly means I was overwhelmed by a constant barrage of beauty queens, nymphomaniacs or Mensa members. Although any or all of those would have been welcomed, my expectations were a bit more realistic. While certainly hoping for more, I was willing to settle for substantially less. If I was able to eek out an entertaining story describing even the most lackluster evening, I considered the date a success. In other words, the bar was set pretty low even though more than a few women managed to bump into it.

But, truth be told (a standard to which I refuse to be held) every woman I met in person was who she claimed to be or, at the very least, a reasonable facsimile thereof. There were, of course, occasional exaggerations about youthful appearance, less than accurate descriptions of body shape or overstatements about desirable features. Still, most of those slight inaccuracies were both predictable and understandable. For the most part, the women who showed up were the women I expected to meet – give or take a few pounds, years or cosmetic surgeries.

The interactions, meetings and events I've included are not chronological or in any other reasonable sequence. My life was pretty random then and not much better organized now. But, because for the most part, the forays into cyberspacial dating came somewhat after the more traditional roads led to dead ends, the online stories are offered later.

At first – and certainly this was more reasonable years ago than it is today – there was justifiable angst about meeting online. But that anxiety proved to be an easy hurdle to clear. There is definitely something exhilarating about finding an e-mail inbox brimming with candidates. Astonishingly there seemed to be a multitude of women who wanted nothing more than to know more about me. Or, as a friend explained, "you're over 40, you're straight and you have a job. You're a "10".

Contrary to some popular misconceptions, the women who participate in online dating sites are by no means limited to desperate losers. As should be evident from many of the e-mail exchanges included in the book, there are a lot of bright, witty, wonderful women who, for any number of reasons, are unattached and looking to share their lives.

I met a lot of them. Some, for reasons that might be considered to be perhaps a bit uncomplimentary, were less memorable than others.Undoubtedly, some were not particularly enthusiastic about me.

My personal journey was filled to the overflowing with missteps, missed opportunities and a plethora of Miss Wrongs. But viewed from the right perspective, quite often the more uncomfortable the situation, the more worthwhile the retelling.

## Getting started is the first step towards getting started

For me, the first decision was unquestionably the hardest. Like everyone else, I'd heard a lot about online dating. I knew people who tried it and even a few who enjoyed at least a modicum of success. But the thought of actually diving into cyberspace all by myself was, to say the least, more than a bit intimidating.

I was well aware that the longest journey begins with the first step. But I was having difficulty figuring out who would take that first step for me.

Eventually I put on my big boy pants and green lighted myself.

Making the all-important decision to get started was clearly the right place – actually the only place - to begin. And, because I had already successfully cleared that major hurdle, I was ready to take the plunge. After patting myself on the back for my bravery and steadfast decision-making it was time to move on to step number two: picking an internet dating site.

At the time there weren't many, so choosing the one that suited me best wasn't that complicated. With some trepidation, I decided to begin with a free one and then, if necessary, eventually work my way towards the "you get what you pay for" sites.

The next responsibility was creating my Profile. Here's the deal with that:

There's not much that can be done about your actual profile. After all, your face is your face and for good or ill, it's the one you're stuck with. But, when writing your online profile, you can be pretty much anything or anyone you want to be.

It's a bit like the way it works in LA. Quite often the people who take your order and bring your meals in many Los Angeles restaurants do not consider themselves to be waiters, waitresses or servers. Many will confidently tell you that they are writers, actors or filmmakers. That's because in Los Angeles you're not limited to what you actually do for a living – you simply define yourself as who, in a more perfect world, you'd prefer to be.

The same holds true for online Profiles. You can feel free to describe yourself any way you want. After all, no one is checking for accuracy. Well, at least not until they meet you in person. So the way you choose to describe yourself is completely up to you. Nevertheless it probably makes sense to remain somewhat within the bounds of credibility because, with luck, you may eventually end up meeting someone who will expect you to at least bear some resemblance to the person you claimed to be.

## Big decision...should I fudge about my age?

There is certainly merit to the theory that you're only as old as you think you are. But there is even more merit to understanding that no matter what you happen to think, others may see you as just plain old.

The idea of skimming a few years off my chronologic age in order to present a number that is more in keeping with the way I want to be perceived seemed reasonable enough. But how many years could I reasonably shave off?

It was definitely time for a reality check.

Despite the way I felt about myself and the way I wanted to believe that I looked, a brief glance in a well lighted mirror revealed an elderly individual with an appearance somewhat like my own but with less hair and more wrinkles.

It hit me then that if I was about to go fishing in the unchartered waters of the internet it was worthwhile to at least be mindful of the bait. Although I wanted to project a youthful attitude there was, just as importantly, the unhappy fact that the lure was incased in the body of a man who would only see 55 again on an MPG sign.

In other words, even though I felt young, I definitely wasn't. That unhappy realization had become apparent a few years earlier when I attended a high school reunion.

The event took place in a large hall where several other celebrations were happening simultaneously. Whether due to poor signage or my own lack of concentration, I entered the wrong room and found myself surrounded by hordes of the barely mobile. These were not people who had aged gracefully. They were well along on their own personal death marches, shuffling slowly, often aided by canes or walkers.

I had obviously stumbled into something similar to an AARP convention on steroids. As soon as I realized my mistake I back-tracked as quickly as possible. Once outside the old age room, I took a deep breath, composed myself and looked for the Information Board where the evening events were posted. Sadly, I had been in the correct hallway all along. So I re-traced my steps and noticed a small sign outside one of the ballrooms.

"Welcome BHS Graduates". That was my school and, sad to say, it was posted outside the very same room I had been in before.

I entered cautiously and realized, upon close inspection, that a few of the faces bore some semblance of familiarity. These old fogies were indeed my classmates, albeit longer in tooth and much the worse for wear. They had not exactly aged gracefully but there was no question that they had aged.

I learned many important things that evening – mostly about lengthy recoveries from operations, the best remedies for back pain, the importance of a knowing a doctor willing to write unlimited prescriptions and where to purchase a custom walker at a very good price. I also saw wallet-sized photos of grandchildren whose cuteness was impossible to describe in spite of the fact that there were many attempts to provide those explanations.

About a month later I received a large envelope containing candid photographs taken at the celebration. Not surprisingly, I was in several of the photos. But surprisingly – at least to me – was my appearance. I looked, not as I had imagined like the spring chicken in the henhouse, but much too much like I belonged there – just as decrepit, withered and ancient as everyone else.

The lesson: assuming that appearance matters – as, of course it regrettably does – then there were limits to the age range of women for whom I might hold some appeal. And, just as importantly, there was an age range for which I need not apply. Thinking young was probably a good thing. But claiming to actually be young was probably a mistake.

Duly noted and so recorded on my Profile.

## Creating a Profile

It's understandable why creating a Profile is intimidating for a lot of people. Describing yourself in a way that is both reasonably accurate and yet still appealing is a daunting task.

But help is readily available. All of the dating websites offer suggestions about what to say in order to elicit responses. I never read any of those suggestions but I have read many more than my share of Profiles. And what is painfully obvious is that either the advice being offered is pretty miserable or it's very good advice that is totally ignored.

In almost every case, even if there is hardly anything included in the Profile, the lack of imagination is almost breathtaking.

By actual count (OK, I never actually counted) it seems that almost every woman includes this information in the description of herself:

I like moonlit walks on the beach
I like to travel
I like to dress up but I'm comfortable in jeans and a sweatshirt I enjoy going out but I'm happing snuggling on the couch, watching old movies
I appreciate fine restaurants but I also love to stay home and cook
My kids are great and my grandkids are even greater

It's amazing how many words can be used to convey almost nothing even remotely interesting or revealing.

Either these women really were boring or their goal was to offend no one. By doing that, I assume they felt they'd get more responses. Mathematically, that may be correct. But for me, the formula didn't make any sense. I wasn't looking for a slew of potential mismatches. I wanted to be more selective: only contenders need apply.

So I put it all out there. This is who I am: an extremely left wing atheist who thinks that brains and a sense of humor are not just high priorities, they're necessities of life.

I wasn't asking that anyone agree with me. I wasn't trying to convince anyone that I was right. All I wanted to communicate was what was important to me. I figured that if we weren't on the same wavelength, a match was unlikely.  So why waste each other's time?
Apparently that is not the suggested method to encourage hordes of responses from eligible women.  But, surprisingly, a number of them did.

Here's my profile. Followed by what happened after I posted it.

# My Profile

*This is the Profile I placed online when I lived in New York. Several years later, as I moved to Delaware and then Philadelphia, my Profile was updated. I added years to correct my advancing age and other pertinent facts about where I lived, vacationed and misspent my waking hours. The exaggerations, however, remained unchanged.*

**"Rich, Handsome, Exaggerator"**

**I Am:** A 59-year-old Male
**Living In:**    New York City, NY
**Seeking:**    Female for a serious relationship
**Height:** 5' 8"
**Body Style:**  Average (I'm surprisingly fit)
**Race/Ethnicity:**    White
**Religion:**    Jewish by birth but aggressively non-religious
**Education:**  Graduate School
**Occupation:** retired
**Income:**    $100,000 or more
**Marital Status:**    Divorced
**Has Children:**    Yes (2 grown sons (24 and 26))
**Wants Children:**    No
**Drinking:**  Drink Occasionally
**Smoking:**  Don't Smoke
**Will Travel:** 5 Miles

**More On Me**

**What celebrity do people say you resemble?**

I have the same number of arms and legs as Paul Newman but surprisingly enough I've never been mistaken for him. Go figure.

**What do you like to do?**

I'm very big on conversation. If the person who is talking is either very smart or very funny, I'm a happy man. If the person is both, I'm thrilled. And if that person is also the woman in my life, I'm delirious with pleasure. I can't say that I like films – I either love them or hate them. Usually, they disappoint me. I'm always up for live jazz, off-Broadway shows, dance (more as an observer than a participant), flea markets, new restaurants, and hanging with friends. I don't cook, but I do dishes. I travel well in America, but don't do nearly as well where English isn't the first language (that would include Europe, Asia, Latin America and most of the Southern States).

**Some of my favorite musicians/albums...**

Nina Simone, Randy Newman, Leon Redbone, Leonard Cohen, Etta James, Bob Dylan, Miles, Brubeck, Monk, Bird.

**I'd also like to say...**

Even though I'm 59, if you stand far enough away and squint, I can easily pass for 58 and 3/4.

For the greater part of my professional life I've been with advertising agencies (usually as a senior executive or a partner). For a while, when I lived in Hollywood, I wrote films and sitcoms. Some were produced - none to my level of satisfaction. I retired from the rat race at the stroke of the millennium (I figured that the rats had already won). Ever since then I've been trying to figure out what I want to be when I grow up. But I'm fairly certain that I no longer want to be a cowboy, a pig farmer or a Trappist Monk.

I still do some business consulting, I'm writing a screenplay and a book, I'm working on a TV pilot, I'm interested in teaching college, I want to travel around the country doing interviews for a documentary, and I'm raising cockroaches in my apartment (you'd be surprised how easy it is to do that).

**Personal Thought or Quote...**
It is better to be rich and healthy than to be poor and sick.

**My Match**

**Age:**   40 to 80-years-old
**Height:** 4' 2" to 7' 2"
**Body Style:**  No Preference

# This is what happened

I had no idea what to expect. But, surprisingly, things did.

Every day I checked to see if I had piqued anyone's interest. Apparently I had. Some wrote to me and, quite often, I wrote back.

Sometimes the email exchanges ended quickly; sometimes they went on for quite a while. If there was sufficient interest, sometimes the digital communication gave way to telephone conversations. And on occasion there were actual in-person meetings.

The stories often developed in unpredictable ways even though the outcome was almost a certainty. I realized that, although hope may spring eternal, there was slim likelihood that I'd find a match made in cyber heaven.

But, as the saying goes, you can't get a hit if you don't swing the bat.

Here are some of my swings and misses. Although I doubt if any of the women remember or care, names have been changed along with some of the specifics. The gist, however, remains pretty much intact.

In an act of unkindness, the emails reprinted here (both mine and theirs) are mostly duplicates of the originals and, as such, include typos, misspellings and errors of grammar.

There is no "Mercy Rule" in cyberspace.

# Carol

*Hi. I was browsing through the love@aol personals (comparing them with the ones I've read on another online service I've been using) and yours caught my eye. I like your picture and like your words. I can't show you a photo (no scanner, and anyhow I think I look better in real life) but have been told many times how attractive I am . . . I'm 47 (look younger--have been told that many times too), 5/8", curly brown hair, green eyes, quite slim, work in book publishing, have been single 2 years after dissolving a 13-year relationship. Love to walk, love jazz, love going to movies (OK, so they're often disappointing--hope springs eternal), love to cook and bake (and feed people I like), still love New York after 10 years here. Love a man who likes to talk and can make me laugh. I think I meet most of your requirements. If you think you might be interested, we could chat. . . Quiz me.*

*Carol*


**Note:**

Her second email came almost immediately – even before I responded the first one)


**2nd from Carol**

*Hi. I realize I told you in my earlier email that I'm 5/8", which would be five-eighths of an inch tall. Maybe you LIKE really short women? But actually I'm five feet, seven inches tall--just not a very good typist. You'd think a person in the publishing business would proofread a little more carefully, wouldn't you?*

Hi Tiny -

Thanks for calling my attention to the height differential. I was actually hoping that the first measurement was correct - I figure I could save a lot of money putting you in my pocket and sneaking you into movies. And, even in a fancy restaurant, at under an inch tall, how much could you possibly eat?

Interesting that you feel you look better in real life than in photos. Most people feel precisely the opposite. With good lighting, correct posing, a skilled photographer and substantial re-touching, anybody can look good in a picture. It's a lot more difficult to hide unwanted features in person. So you get high marks for confidence. I, on the other hand, would prefer to be viewed in a wallet-sized full body photo, preferably taken in a dimly lit room. Perhaps we could introduce my itty bitty shot to your 5/8" woman.

So, where were you before you came to NY and took on the publishing world? What kind of publishing? What do you do in the field?

Answers to those questions are not mandatory. Feel free to ignore them completely. I was just trying to learn some more about you. Anything you want to offer is more than fine with me.

I look forward to hearing from you.

Howie

*Hi, Howie.*

*My spell checker suggests changing your name to Whoopie, Howell, Hawaii or Hopi.*

*OK, so I'm taller than I let on. I'm still a pretty cheap date. Actually I've spent a lot of energy over the years trying to be tall and thin, and I finally seem to have made it. I visited my father recently and he said he was sure I'd gotten taller. Of course, this may just mean that he's getting shorter. Do you know that scene in The Big Sleep where Humphrey Bogart meets Lauren Bacall's little nymphet sister? She looks at him and says, "You're not very tall." He says, "I try to be."*

*But enough on the subject of height. Before I came to NYC, I was a Minnesotan, and I lived in Tallahassee for three years too. Why Tallahassee, of all places, you may be asking yourself. Funny, I'm still asking myself. The short answer is that I went with my then boyfriend, who got a teaching job at Florida State. Those were strange three years. I don't know if you've ever lived in the South . . . Tallahassee is in north Florida, and there's a saying down there that Florida is the only state that gets more Southern the farther north you go.*

*Anyhow. I've been in New York ten years, as I think I said. I work in children's and young adult books--I manage a copyediting department. A lot of people don't even know what a copy editor is, but since you're a writer, I'm sure you do. And I hope you won't hold it against me. It's an interesting job, although not always the stroll in the park you might think it would be. As you may have heard, in children's publishing, it's bunny eat bunny.*

*Basic info, just to be fair: I have a B.A. (from a little liberal arts school in Iowa), have a Catholic mother and a Jewish father (oh, the guilt!), am like you pretty aggressively nonreligious, have a brother who lives nearby in New Jersey*

60

*and a sister in Minnesota, have never been married, don't drink much at all and never smoke.*

*That's enough out of me for now, I think. What do you think?*

*Carol*


Hi Carol -

My spell checker offered no substitutes for your name. Does it mean that mine is more forgiving than yours or that it's simply not interested? Of the names yours suggested, I'm most partial to Whoopie (sounds both enthusiastic and a little risqué).

I know very little about Tallahassee. Here's the sum total of my knowledge about the city and Florida State: the head of the philosophy department is a college friend. He and I were the only two philosophy majors at the tiny school we attended in North Carolina (see, I know something about the South, too).

Your analysis of the South somewhat parallels mine. It took me all four years of college to get over my prejudice about Southerners. I eventually came to realize that despite their accents, some of them actually were smart and some of them could even think. Then, after graduation, it took about a minute and a half for all of my prejudices to return. It is, unquestionably, my least favorite part of America.

So, you want to know what I think? I think you sound terrific. You obviously have the smart and funny parts covered, and as far as matters of personal tastes are concerned, I have always favored slender women who are less than 5'8" and more than 1/2" in height.

61

If you feel like moving to the phone call plateau, here's my number:   000-000-0000 Or we could keep on writing. Your choice.

Howie


**Note:**

What happened after has long escaped my memory. I assume that Carol and I spoke on the phone or possibly even met for coffee or dinner. For reasons that have long since faded, magic never happened or both of us saw the Dead End sign fast approaching.

It was fun while it lasted. But it didn't last.

# Caroline

*Subject: Hi*

*You sound very interesting, and, more importantly to me, funny. Are we a potential match? Match.com sent you to me as a match so who am I to argue with their divine intervention? Now it's up to you to risk upsetting the cosmos.*

*Caroline*


Hi Caroline –

My guess is that Match.com will be pleased that you have elevated them to deity status. It's probably a loftier position than intended. I think their process is a little less cosmic – their theory seems to be that if two people both have a similar quantity of their own teeth, they're ideally suited.

Shall we continue?

Howie


## Note:

We did continue with a few relatively lackluster exchanges. Most of them are missing but few will be missed. Apparently – and not surprisingly – in an email Caroline felt that I offered some information that she deemed to be less than appropriate. It generated this response:

*Hi*

*Maybe because it's late and I'm very tired or maybe because cyberspace communicating isn't really communicating at all... but I'm not sure I understand what you're saying. I really wasn't trying to insult your intelligence with any of the ridiculous things I said. Just didn't know how to take your responses to my email. Is this our lover's quarrel even though we'll probably never meet? If you would like to talk in real time I'm game. If this is goodbye, then, good bye.*

*Caroline*


Miss C –

A quarrel requires, at the very least, two people. So, by actual head count, we're missing one.

I didn't feel insulted by your email and I certainly didn't intend to start a battle with mine. Perhaps if you re-read it with a large smile and a well-rested mind, you may note at least a hopeful hint of humor.

Nevertheless, you are of course, correct about the difficulty caused by communicating through interfacing computers. Often, what is intended as playful banter ends up seeming hurtful, angry or just plain mean.

If you'd like to get on with a conversation aimed towards setting the lover's spat, I'm up for that.

Here's my home phone number:  000-000-0000. If you don't call, how will we ever get to make-up sex?

Howie

*Subject: Hi*

*I never called because life got in the way - everything from a birth to a death. Neither mine. Is it too late now?*

*Caroline*


Miss Caroline –

Finally, I can abandon my phone-side vigil. Finally there is an answer to the question, "Why hasn't she called? Why? Why? Why?"

Now, after lo' these many months, all is clear. What seemed to be a deep, meaningful relationship built on trust, mutual understanding and a shared sense of compassion now turns out to be something so trivial it could be cast aside by minor incidents like birth, death and other unmentionables that possibly include a Mid-East Disturbance and the desperate need to locate a cure for hangnails. In your absence, I had no choice but to turn to others for solace, support and sexual satisfaction. The all-too obvious result – herpes, open sores, loss of self-esteem, a tragic dip in my personal fortune and, worst of all, misplacement of my lucky garlic press – has brought me to the precipice. I lay here curled around the well worn teddy bear that has been my only trusted friend, confidant and advisor as I attempt to carry on.

On the bright side, there seems to be little angst over the total collapse of the world economy, there are still millions who fervently, albeit unaccountably, believe that Sarah Palin is eminently qualified to be President and, happily the milk in my refrigerator has not soured even though the Sell By date has long since passed.

After abandoning hope, I have been able to pick up the pieces and move on. The woman who now shares my life, despite her stutter and somewhat curious devotion to witchcraft, has proven totally capable of manipulating her electric wheelchair with great aplomb. Soon we will be off to seek our fortune as either bounty hunters or toll collectors at a yet-to-be-constructed bridge.

Alas, Sweet Caroline, our time has come and, regrettably, gone.

I wish you whatever you wish that I wish you.

Howie

# Genie

**Note:**

Genie responded to my Match.com Profile. I no longer have that response nor do I remember very much about what she wrote. It was, however, sufficiently interesting to generate a reply - quite possibly because of a reference to a villa in Italy that she once owned and the fact that she signed her note "Sophie Tucker 77".

We began a relatively consistent and lengthy email conversation that, upon re-reading, was less than fascinating. Accordingly, in an act of kindness, most of it has been removed. Only the mediocre parts remain.

You're welcome.


Hi -

I'm going to take a wild guess and assume that your name really isn't Sophie Tucker and that the "77" refers to neither to your age nor your wingspan.

And your Profile isn't really a profile either. It's a full frontal head and shoulders photo. A fine one at that but, nevertheless, not a profile.

With luck, there will be a photo either attached or imbedded in this email.

I have no clever pseudonym. Most people call me Howie. Probably because that's my name.

I'm up for more if you are.

Howie

*hey...*

*thank u for noticing my profile (or as u pointed out... my not a profile)...and 4 writing.*

*It sounds like u have had an interesting life so far. what are you doing now that life is unstructured and u have to make your days up out of whole cloth?*

*I retired early (don't you HATE that word) ... and have since returned to the pleasant and soul feeding work of art.. i have a BFA but i feel i reallllly never learned to paint so this is a new life for me...and i am loving it.*

*–genie*

Hi Genie -

So there is a name after all - combined with an unusual spelling. I will bow to discretion and omit any clever reference to bottles and wishes. Oops, it got out anyway.

I really did retire early. It was my company - well, there were other partners, too - but when I left it was because I simply didn't want to be there anymore. In other words, I downsized myself.

Thanks for responding so quickly. It's always difficult to participate in a one-way communication.

Howie

P.S.

Is painting something you do for fun, for remuneration, or because you finally have the time? There are times when I write simply because I need the relief that it brings. And, there are times when my writing serves no purpose other than to amuse me.

Howie (Again. Still.)


*hi howie...*

*how was your week. i have been a bit on the run.... yesterday i spent a good part of the day at scott honda in west chester. i just got a CRV and had to take it in because i couldn't open the tailgate lock with the key...turns out i am an ass :( just had to turn the key harder..... yikes! but i had them do a slight wheel alignment too so it was worth the trip...and i got to spend a few hours with an 'art friend' who lives out that way.*

*-genie*


Hi Genie -

Good to hear from you.

I think the way they fixed your car is a perfect example of one my rules for living: when in doubt, force it. The result is predictable. Either the thing will work or you'll feel justified in breaking it. And, at that point, you can usually come up with a few choice words that not only release frustration, but also pass the blame on to an inanimate object.

Now that you're no longer chained to a desk in the corporate world, are you living off of your vast inheritance, the incredible fees you charge for your paintings or have you cut back on your life style and limited your trips abroad as well as your semi-annual vacations at the Tuscan villa?

69

Time to get myself in gear for tonight's dinner. A few minor errands need running and, given that these are relatively new friends, I may even take a shower.

Howie


*H –*


*oh wow a shower affair tonight...good 4 u! here's what i have unfortunately found... regarding get-togethers with friends'... the men do get invited to the dinner parties and picnics etc. maybe alone maybe there is a fix-up but a single woman can go hang herself before she is welcome in many private mixed situations. it's unfortunate but women do not like to have single women around and available i think.*
*let me know how the dinner party goes. i may be having a dinner party too... chinese food with my son and ex. haha strange world.*

*-genie*


Hi Genie -

Turns out the shower was kinda wasted. With all the rain last night and today, I could have simply walked outside with a bar of soap.

I've not shared your experience with single men vs. single women as invitees to social situations. My feeling is that we live in a family world and a couple's world and that singles of either sex live just a bit on the periphery. Sometimes they are included but more often they are not. And, for some singles, attending an event where everyone else is paired off somehow feels uncomfortable. Which may account for the lack of invitations or the lack of accepting those invitations on the rare occasions when they are offered. Still, I don't disagree that being a single woman can be difficult. I can only assume that for some wives, keeping a husband of many years interested is tough enough without having an unattached, attractive woman adding to the difficulty.

You said that you were attaching a charcoal drawing. Perhaps you didn't glue it to the email with the proper fixative. But, just because I was unable to see it doesn't mean I am unable to comment. In true art-speak review, "I found the work an intensive blend of line and movement which distilled a sense of energy and calm into divergent, yet representative dualities."

Having Chinese food with your son last night sounds like a great idea. Having the same meal with your ex sounds a bit peculiar, but as long as everyone's fine with the company, why not? My ex and I are in little danger of sharing meals since she still lives in LA.

You ready to up the ante? If you are, here's my phone number:   000 000-0000. A rainy day phone call might be just the thing to bring some sunshine into an otherwise pretty dreary day.

Howie

*hi howie...*

*i appreciate your pithy words on my invisible charcoal haha   ...i will attach a  different picture...a pastel from a photo i took in Times Square recently.  i thought it was very amusing and called it "The Un-freeway."*

*i am taking a critique class(a whole other story) in chadds ford tuesdays and after class i have to get my teeth cleaned ... i don't know which is worse.*
*g.*

Miss G –

Is it possible to combine activities and have the dental hygienist simply critique your teeth? Just a thought.

Tomorrow I'm in New York to finish editing a film I did for the Delaware Theatre Co. Hopefully the work won't take long and I'll be able to squeeze in at least one decent meal and some evening entertainment as well. Frankly, I'm much better at eating and being entertained that I am at editing.

Mr. Howie


*hey editor man..... so how was nyc?   did u get done what u went to do?  how did u get to ny...train?   did u taste any big apple night life?   i think i may be the only person in america who doesn't really like broadway musicals.   i saw phantom last year when i was visiting Sheila...could take it or leave it.*

*now if i had seen swimming to cambodia....*

*-g*


Miss G -

Well, there are at least two of us who have difficulty with Broadway musicals. As a matter of fact, I can't take much of Broadway at all. I like unusual plays, I like the experimental stuff, and I'm up for seeing plays that aren't mainstream.  But you'd have to rope and tie me up to get me to see a musical. I did see Hedwig and the Angry Inch - but it was hardly mainstream theatre. The music was interesting - and actually quite good - but the production was fabulous. It wouldn't have lasted a minute on Broadway because the blue haired ladies would have hated every second.

I didn't see Swimming to Cambodia on stage - but I did see the video. Last year - about 6 months before he committed suicide - I saw Spalding Gray at the Grand Opera house in Wilmington. The show was wonderful – but I had no idea how unhappy he really was.

Enjoy the rain. Looks like it's gonna be here for awhile.

Mr. Howie

*MR. Howie –*

*there is something big and bright and hot and scarey outside today in the sky...what IS that? I actually have the tape of swimming to cambodia.... or maybe it is monster in a box when spalding grey committed suiside i was shocked, i too had no idea. he is so quick and so brilliant and has been an important person on the political/writing/commentary/theater scene for so long. it was very sad.*

*G*

Miss G -

Don't know what sky you're looking at - over here it's bright, beautiful and blue with lots of big puffy clouds. That ought to last at least another 15 minutes and then the rains will surely be back again.

OK. Here's the deal. We can keep on doing emails for as long as you want. I love to write - and I do it everyday. It's part of what makes me happy. So as long as you're up for continuing as electronic pen pals, I'll be right with you. But I think it's time to take the risk of voice contact. But it takes two people to have a conversation and if you don't want to go there, that's OK. It just seems like the next logical step.

So here, again, is my phone number. 000-000-0000. You can do it. Just take a deep breath and push the buttons.

Howie


*H –*
*you r such a witty and wise person and a terriffic writer! i'm not going to go thru a litany of reasons i think men drop off the face of cyber space but i could.*

*here's the thing: i sense we have a good potential for a terriffic friendship. i am not really fond of talking on the phone especially to people i haven't met, i find it awkward and hate all teh question asking(for lack of what to talk about).*

*i will leave it up to u if u want to write now and then. i would expect not. it has been a treat to have corresponded with you.*

*-genie*


Hi Genie -

Here's what you wrote. My response is in ALL CAPS.

you r such a witty and wise person and a terrific writer! i'm not going to go thru a litany of reasons i think men drop off the face of cyber space but i could.

TRUTHFULLY, I'D LOVE TO KNOW YOUR THOUGHTS ABOUT WHY MEN DROP OFF THE FACE OF CYBER SPACE. I CAN THINK OF A LOT OF REASONS. BUT I CAN'T THINK OF ONE THAT'S ANY BETTER THAN WHEN THE OTHER PERSON SHUTS DOWN COMPLETELY. COMMUNICATION IS A TWO WAY STREET. IT'S KIND OF DIFFICULT TO HAVE A ONE-WAY CONVERSATION - EVEN VIA THE INTERNET.

here's teh thing: i sense we have a good potential for a terriffic friendship. i am not really fond of talking on teh phone especially to people i haven't met, i find it awkward and hate all teh question asking(for lack of what to talk about).
i will leave it up to u if u want to write now and then. i would expect not. it has been a treat to have corresponded with you.

-genie


I THINK IT'S TOO EARLY TO KNOW IF WE HAVE THE POTENTIAL FOR A TERRIFIC FRIENDSHIP. WAY TOO EARLY. BUT IF WE DON'T COMMUNICATE, IT WILL BE IMPOSSIBLE TO FIND OUT. IF YOU BELIEVE THERE ARE LIMITATIONS TO FRIENDSHIP - THAT, FOR EXAMPLE, A TERRIFIC FRIENDSHIP IS POSSIBLE IF THE FRIENDS ONLY WRITE TO EACH OTHER, I THINK YOU'RE WRONG. WRITING CAN COMMUNICATE A LOT. BUT TALKING CAN COMMUNICATE A LOT TOO. AND, BEING IN THE SAME PHYSICAL SPACE CAN COMMUNICATE A SIGNIFICANT AMOUNT - EVEN WITHOUT CONVERSATION.

THE REASON I WANTED TO TALK ON THE PHONE IS TO DETERMINE (FOR BOTH YOU AND ME) IF THERE IS REASON TO BELIEVE THAT A FRIENDSHIP IS POSSIBLE. THAT'S WHAT I MEANT BY "TAKING IT UP A NOTCH." LIMITING COMMUNICATION TO EMAILS - ESPECIALLY AT THIS TIME - IS ALSO PUTTING A LIMIT ON THE FRIENDSHIP.

TALKING ON THE PHONE WITH PEOPLE YOU HAVEN'T MET DOESN'T HAVE TO BE PAINFUL. NOR DOES IT REQUIRE A BRUTAL QUESTION AND ANSWER SESSION. CONVERSATIONS ARE ABOUT THE SHARING OF INFORMATION - BUT THE SUBJECTS OF THOSE DISCUSSIONS CAN BE PRETTY OPEN ENDED. AND THE QUALITY, HUMOR, DEPTH, AND VALIDITY OF WHAT IS

COMMUNICATED HAS THE SAME POTENTIAL FOR DISASTER OR SUCCESS AS DOES THE WRITING OF EMAILS.

TO SUM UP:

IF YOU WANT THE SAFETY AND DETACHMENT OF A FRIENDSHIP THAT EXISTS ONLY IN CYBERSPACE, THEN IT'S TIME TO STOP.  TO ME, IT MEANS THAT YOU'VE PLACED A LID ON THE POTENTIAL FOR THE QUALITY OF THE FRIENDSHIP.  I'M MORE THAN HAPPY TO STEP BACK FROM FRIENDSHIPS OR RELATIONSHIPS AT ANY TIME. BUT MY REASONS USUALLY HAVE TO DO WITH AN EVALUATION OF WHAT HAS HAPPENED RATHER THAN BY GUESSING WHAT MIGHT POSSIBLY OCCUR.

THIS IS THE REAL STUFF.  YOU AND I ARE, AT THIS MOMENT, BARELY SNIFFING AROUND IT.  IF YOU WANT TO FIND OUT IF THERE'S MORE HERE THAN MEETS THE COMPUTER, I'M UP FOR DOING THE DANCE A LITTLE LONGER - AT LEAST UNTIL TOO MANY TOES ARE TROD UPON.

BUT IF YOU FEEL THAT THE ZENITH OF A FRIENDSHIP WITH ME HAS ALREADY HIT ITS CYBERSPACIAL CEILING, THEN IT'S TIME FOR ME SAY GOODBYE.

HOWIE

*howie,*

*there is an art director in Erie; we have been writing for several years. i think we talked on the phone twice, his voice seemed high pitched and i am not attracted to him romantically (which i can tell from photos ) but we have a lot in common and are always honest and supportive and open having much to say particularly about art. i would call him a friend. if he lived closer we'd be visiting galleries and talking 'art' over coffee.*

*i could never have enuf of these 'friends'. do you have people like this in your life?*

*-g*

Miss G –

I get it. I'm often slow, occasionally dense, and sometimes just plain obtuse.

But I do get it. You don't wanna talk. OK. I don't know why, but the message is clear.

Nevertheless, and for no reason save my own amusement (and perhaps yours) I have tried to 'suss it out. So here are my top ten guesses about why Genie doesn't want to call.

1. She paints, she writes, but she doesn't actually speak. Frankly, it's a poor excuse. Lots of guys would kill for a relationship with a mute woman.

2. All of the summer money for household services has gone into air conditioning and car repair. The telephone is hooked up but non-functioning until the bill is paid.

3. Dyslexia makes dialing an exercise in frustration. Getting all 10 digits in the proper sequence requires such

extreme effort that, upon completion, you would be too exhausted to communicate.

4. Talking on the phone is the next step down the slippery slope from which there is no return. To wit: writing, talking, meeting, relationship, marriage, dysfunction, co-dependency, and the eventual acrimonious divorce.

5. You fear that I possess either a videophone or X-ray vision and am therefore able to see the additional 75 pounds gained since the posted photograph was taken.

6. You are, in fact, Sophie Tucker and your voice quality would give that away in a second. It would also prove that you were inaccurate in describing your age because Sophie is not only deceased but also 112 years old.

7. Your calling plan does not include the 000 area code which would mean there is a possibility that conversation would not only be disappointing, but also end up costing you a buck seventy five.

8. You are certain that I not only have Caller ID, but also, because of my affiliation with the CIA, FBI, and the crackerjack Wilmington Police Department, am able to triangulate and track the exact location of the telephone so that by the time the call has ended I could be on your doorstep delivering pizza - probably with anchovies.

9. You really wanted to call, intended to call, and had every inclination to call but your schedule makes such an act impossible. After all, there are teeth to brush, clothes to put on and lord knows someone had to scan the sky for the potentiality of rain.

10. As a joke, somebody crazy-glued the telephone to the wall and when you attempted to lift the receiver the entire house came crashing down. You were immediately rushed to the hospital but, in the excitement, neglected to bring my phone number.

**Note:**

This next email from me was a bonus. My previous one was certainly sufficiently clear. But, for reasons I don't remember and certainly can't justify, I decided to send a final one.

Miss G -

You ask if I have any friends similar to your art director in Erie. Hard to say. I have lots of friends all over the country - and some in other parts of the world - that I do not see regularly. With some I maintain a telephone relationship. With others I do email. And with others I don't communicate at all - until we get together. All of my friends - those I contact regularly and those who only appear infrequently are important to me. Almost without exception, the friendships I've made have sprung out of physical meetings. We've worked together, lived near each other, gone to school together, met through other friends, met through our kids, attended a party, participated in an event or shared some sort of experience. The relationships evolved from there.

I have lots of friends like that. I anticipate making more friends in similar ways. But, frankly, I'm not looking for an email relationship that lives exclusively in cyberspace. I do understand, however, that's precisely what you are hoping to find.

I'm looking for a real relationship. One that would include things like talking, laughing, touching and probably a lot more intimacy than you seem able to handle. You're not wrong for wanting what you want. I'm not wrong for wanting what I want. But clearly we are on very different paths.

You seem to be a kind and generous person. I wish you happiness. But it's obvious that I will not be someone who fosters or shares it with you.

Howie

# Kimberly

**Note:**

I responded to a Profile that Kimberly posted on Match.com. That response - brilliant, witty and informative though it may have been – is missing. All that is known for certain is that my note was sufficient to generate a response from her. Thus began an interchange – and much of that has disappeared as well. Nevertheless, the narrative picks up here with Kimberly's email:

*Dear H (hope you don't mind my using your first name.*
*After all, we hardly know each other.*

*What can I say to someone who writes such an*
*articulate, humorous note, someone whose SATs must*
*have been reasonably high even if he can't remember.*
*If you'd added that you can cook, I'd have said there*
*IS a God!*

*Glad you decided to return to NY, where integrity*
*Occasionally reigns.  As far as saving France, though,*
*I thought Jerry Lewis had already taken care of that.*
*Don't worry, though - rumor has it that Staten Island is*
*still up for saving.*

*I just returned from a trip to Thailand and Vietnam.*
*My draft number finally came up!  Aside from the*
*occasional captured U.S. tank on the side of the road,*
*Saigon looked like any other capitalist Asian city.*
*The first time someone asked where I was from,*
*I thought uh oh, better look for the exit. But people*
*were surprisingly friendly & welcoming. Twenty five*
*years does a lot.*

*I work for financial advisors, but I'm not at all the
Wall Street type -- I had a rather bohemian upbringing
& it hasn't altogether disappeared. So my firm
tolerates me as their token left winger.*

*As far as selling your email address to infidels, the
guys at www.infidel.org said they already have it, so
until I find another group that's interested, your
secret is safe with me.*

*As you can probably tell, I enjoy writing, but in the
interest of saving time, what would you say to using
the phone lines for their original purpose -- to have
a conversation? Let me know.*

*Kimberly*


Miss K –

You can call me H anytime. It almost makes me sound like
an adult. If you have time for an extra syllable you could
call me Howard. Or, with the same amount of energy you
could call me Howie - which is what everyone else does.

Sorry about the answer I'm about to give to the "are you a
wonderful cook" question. No… But I can heat up. I can
order out.  I can bring home and plate appropriately. Or, I
can do what I prefer most - go to my sources (usually
Zagat) and make sure you're fed well or well fed, whichever
comes first.  Does that mean there is a God?  Well, if She
takes plastic...

Thailand and Viet Nam - wow. Not exactly the same as
vacationing at Club Med. I have some friends who make
annual pilgrimages to Thailand. Don't know if it's the drugs,
the people or the prices that keeps them coming back. I
think it's probably a combination of all three.

Last year I saw an amazing film by an American woman whose husband was killed in the Vietnamese War. She made a documentary - interviewing other war widows, both in America and Viet Nam (where, not surprisingly, they refer to it as the "American War"). It was, as you might expect, a pretty powerful work, made all the more so by the very thing you described - the accepting, welcoming and friendly (not to mention forgiving) people of Viet Nam.

Sure, I'm up for telephonic communication. To prove it, here's my number: 000-000-0000. But tomorrow (Monday) may not be a perfect day - I have meetings in the afternoon and a dinner that could run fairly late. Still, my guess is that I'll be home by 10 - which would be a fine time for a phone call. Actually, any time you feel like calling would be fine. I'm usually up pretty late, and I get funnier as my brain gets fuzzier.

Howie


**Note:** Another email exchange is missing. But through brilliant deductive reasoning, it appears that, based on my response, Kimberly has admitted, boasted or merely offered the prideful information that she participates in Ballroom Dance Competitions.

Another salient piece of information that seems obvious is that she was going to Montana for a while. The story picks up when she returns.


*Dear H,*

*I'm back! And am here to say they really do wear cowboy hats out there. (We don't care if it is 98 degrees, we're real men!) Forest fires are blazing like crazy. I hope there's some forestland and animals left after all this. I also went to the last brothel in Montana, which was closed in 1982 by an*

*old-fogey mayor. While I was on the little tour, a real*
*western-type fistfight broke out between two locals. Time*
*Magazine was there to do an article -- it's in this week's*
*issue. I'm going to pick one up to see if my picture made it.*
*(Fame at last, even if it is in a brothel.)*

*So if Ms. Right hasn't stumbled across your path in her 5*
*inch backless platform shoes, give me a call.  000-000-0000*

*Kim*


Hiya Kim  -

It's not hard for me to picture you in a brothel - at least no
harder than to picture you anyplace else.  The only specific
image I can conjure up is a woman dressed to the Nines for
a Ballroom Dancing Competition. Many of those dresses
would not make it into a traditional PG movie...even a
movie about hookers.

Cowboy hats, ridiculous though they may be, are worn in
way too many places in America. Texas, even in the cities,
seems to encourage strange attire. Most Texans don't wear
spurs anymore, but they are mighty proud of their hats and
boots.

While you were gone, no one knocked on my door wearing
the shoes you described. Pity. Do you have such 5-inch
backless platform shoes? Do they have stiletto heels? Do
you have the rest of the outfit, which, I assume, would
include ripped net stockings and a large flower in your hair?

In theory there is now a message on your machine. It
should say something incredibly witty. Something like:
"let's get together." Call me at 000-000-0000.

Howie (H)

**Note:**

There is no happy or sad ending to the Kimberly experience. All there is an ending.

Based on the very positive tone of our exchanged emails, I can only assume that we spoke on the phone and, quite possibly, even met in person. But there are a few memory lapses. For example I don't remember what Kimberly looked like, where she lived or, most importantly, where or how the disconnect occurred.

For convenience sake, let's put it all on her. She was too tall (or too short), poorly dressed (or over-dressed) and wore too little or far too much inappropriate make-up.

She may have been unable to adequately explain the need for a parole officer to accompany her when we met. She may have been embarrassingly inept at handling chopsticks or perhaps even a knife and fork. She may have examined the menu and in a fit of glee, exclaimed "they have soup d' jour...it's my favorite!"

Or – and this is most likely – she was much too quick to assess my very few and very minor faults.

One way or the other the Kimberly saga concluded. Best guess: not with a bang and probably not even with a whimper - just a mutually agreed upon goodbye and good luck.

# Penny

**Note:**

Penny started the ball rolling with a short response to my Match.com posting. Essentially she asked if I was up for a conversation. After what I assume was a review of her Profile, I was game to take the next step.

Hi Penny –

Let the banter begin.

My next response may be slightly delayed because at noon I'm leaving the safety of the city for a day at the Salem County Fair in New Jersey. If it's anything like last year, it will be as ridiculous as you think. After an afternoon of stimulating intellectual activities involving pig racing, pie judging and tractor pulling, I'll be spending the night and dining with friends as far from the barnyard as possible.

But I look forward to our conversation, filtered though it may be through the magic of technology.

Howie

*Hi,*

*Thanks for getting back to me. It sounds like you have a very amusing day ahead. I'm off to my country house in Columbia County tomorrow, but will have internet access. Let's start with your name....*

*Penny*

**Note:** What followed next was….nothing. But, for reasons that escape me now, I was sufficiently interested to make another effort).

Hi Penny –

It's me - Howie - a voice (well, OK, an email) from your recent past.

The last I heard from you, you were going off to Columbia county and then...nothing.

Did you take up permanent residence at your country estate? Are you now involved, married, pregnant, or otherwise engaged? Did my last email not get through, seem unworthy of response or are you no longer interested in email banter or, possibly, something more?

Just curious.

Howie


*Hi,*

*I never heard from you. Perhaps you should contact Match about the lost email - that happens with disturbing frequency. I'm back in the city and headed into a very busy day. Forward me your past email and I'll respond when I get a chance.*

*I just moved into a new house in Bella Vista yesterday, so things are pretty hectic.*

*Penny*

Hi Penny –

Welcome back. Moving, even if it's to much better digs, still comes with frustration, anxiety and an amazing number of boxes. Even so, the worst is over. Unpacking usually doesn't need to be accomplished on a specific schedule. So, if you can, take your time.

Below is what appears to be the lost email:

Miss Penny –

Sorry about the name omission.

Actually, I did type it, saw it at the bottom of my email and felt confident that it would be included along with whatever drivel I managed to impart.

Of all the many things I have to hide (although most of the official charges against me have been dropped due to inadmissible evidence, threats, or sizeable payoffs to amenable judges) my name is the least of my concerns. Officially, it's Howard. But everyone calls me Howie. When I was much younger, that name made sense. Now it's simply absurd. It sounds juvenile, immature and inappropriate for an adult. In other words, it suits me very well.

News from the Salem County Fair. The blue ribbon went to a 3 1/2 pound tomato. I was mightily impressed but it turns out that the woman who raised (grew, fed, over-indulged?) it has won the same award 11 years in a row - often for much larger specimens. Having never even attempted to grow a vegetable, flower or raise anything other than a puppy or my own children, I was monumentally awed. My acute knowledge of farm animals became somewhat suspect during the steer judging. Not once did my choice end up winning, coming in second or even third. Three times in a row - probably somewhat of a County Fair record – I picked the steer that came in dead last. Later in the afternoon when I had the opportunity to talk with the official judge, he saw no humor in my willingness to help him make better choices in the future.

I am now safely returned to the city. Curious that I find nothing appealing in the aromas of swine, goats or sheep but the comforting smell of dog shit on New York sidewalks make me feel right at home.

Howie

(one more time - just to be safe)

Howie


**Note:**

Although it seems inconceivable, apparently Penny did not want to hear any more about County Fairs, livestock winners or oversized tomatoes. Whatever the reason, there were no more emails from her and, just for spite, none from me either.

# Phyllis

*I have a friend on match who says that he has had at least 600 emails in the month since he has joined. If that is true???? then it is probably double for you. Here's one more.*

*I too have come to some of the same religious conclusions. I think there may be "something more" out there but the crap they feed us about this wise old man in the sky thingy can't be right.*

*Well, I know you peeked at my profile. I must like yours better than you liked mine. :-) As far as your turn ons list...I'm okay on the sarcasm but I would hopefully not turn it on you. I'm pretty good on the brains in certain areas. Boldness.........well this email is pretty bold but that may be all there is in that area.*

*Phyllis*

Hi Phyllis-

Thanks for being bold.

I think, by actual count, I've fallen somewhat short of the 1,200 email responses that you projected. Of course, there were hordes of women lining up at my front door, parachuting on to my roof and causing traffic jams throughout the city. I requested that they line up alphabetically, according to height, education level, promiscuity and neediness but the more aggressive ones always seemed to claw their way to the front, completely disregarding rules of decorum and propriety. I am generally not swayed by gifts but I must confess that some of the over-the-top gestures (including the cleverly monogrammed helicopter) were, even for me, difficult to return.

90

Perhaps there is just a wisp of exaggeration in some of those statements. In truth, stating in my Profile that I am a godless heathen surely took its toll. I probably would have eliminated fewer women if I claimed to be an unemployed child molester/wife beater. Curious how the magical adult fairy tales about God, Yahweh, Jehovah, Mohammad and/or the Cookie Monster have been swallowed with such gusto in the U.S. but are almost a non-factor in the UK.

Howie


*Howie:*

*If I send you $.25 for each email, even if we never meet, will you keep emailing me? I do love to laugh. I hope you are now writing your first book!*

*I was wondering how you made out with your statement about Godlessness. Having been raised by a father who was a self proclaimed agnostic, it has been difficult for me to deal with religion. He actually picked up the bible and showed me statements that contradicted themselves. Religion has ruled the world and started wars over the centuries and still does. Just how stupid man/woman is, is pointed out by this issue. Then there is the human/canine issue of territory. I don't know whether religion or territory or the combination have caused more wars. Bottom line, I don't like religion. I am perfectly capable of being a "good" person, whether I am threatened by hell or rebirth as a centipede, or not.*

*Phyl*

Hi Phyl –

If you're going to offer a quarter per email, you should at least set a few requirements. I would suggest that there be a minimum word count, something to indicate that the message has been formulated for you and is not a copy of one that has been generated for the masses and, to be fair, there should be some guarantee about a minimum of guffaws. A less scrupulous person than I might consider adding surcharges for fuel, energy or wear and tear on keyboards. Taxes, especially considering that the content is traveling across state lines, could send the total rocketing towards 30¢ or even higher.

Last night I went to see Randy Newman. His take on religion is similar to ours. Although he didn't sing it last night, his song "That's why I love mankind" is both funny and sad at the same time. It nails the absurdity of our willingness to suspend belief in God in spite of the doom and destruction that we so willingly accept was caused by His hand. (OK, you don't have to pay for this paragraph – definitely not funny).

Big weekend for me. My son and his wife are celebrating their 3rd anniversary and I get to babysit my 10 month old granddaughter. If I'm especially lucky I'll get to change her diaper. After that I'll probably do what I always do – shoot up and go out looking for crack whores.

Here comes further proof that I understand the relationship of services performed vs. money paid. I can stop on a dime.

See?

Howie

*Hi Howie:*

*We will have to work out a legal contract if you decide to take me up on my offer of $.25 per email.*

*Funny, but last weekend it was my daughter's and son in law's 10th anniversary and I had my grandson's over for a sleep over. It was much fun. It was the first time they ever slept here. I am jealous that you have a granddaughter. Maybe my son will finally get married and have one for me. However, babysitting will be expensive since he lives in CA.*

*It is a great day to get things done. I rearranged my kitchen cabinets and made some soup. Tomorrow I have what will probably be a last date with someone I meet on Match. He is definitely not a match. He is very nice but hardly speaks and when he does I think my dogs are more interesting. That's my weekend. I tried to look up that song by Randy Newman but had no luck.*

*Enjoy that baby. My boys (grandsons) are 8 and 6.*

*Phyl*


Miss P –

I have no excuse for being up at this hour but here I am nevertheless. It's way too early for me – especially on a rainy Sunday but as long as I'm up I figured I'd do something useful. This is it.

I think you're judging the guy from Match.com pretty harshly. While you may find your dogs more interesting, comparing men to dogs is certainly a high bar for us males to clear. I once dated a woman who told me that all she wanted in a man was someone who was as excited to see her as her dogs were every time she came home. Turns out, I wasn't that guy.

At 10 months of age, I don't think there is a major difference between little boys and little girls. But, I am excited about my granddaughter – she's the first girl in 4 generations. We are a manly group.

Here are the lyrics to Randy's song. Frankly, like most songs, it's better sung.  But the words are pretty wonderful:

God's Song by Randy Newman

Cain slew Able, Seth knew not why
For if the children of Israel were to multiply
Why must any of the children die?
So he asked the Lord
And the Lord said:

*Man means nothing, he means less to me*
*Than the lowliest cactus flower*
*Or the humblest Yucca tree*
*He chases round this desert*
*Cause he thinks that's where I'll be.*
*That's why I love mankind*
*I recoil in horror from the foulness of thee*
*From the squalor and the filth and the misery*
*Howe we laugh up here in heaven at the prayers you offer me.*
*That's why I love mankind.*

*The Christians and Jews were having a jamboree*
*The Buddhists and the Hindus joined on satellite TV*
*They picked their four greatest priests*
*And they began to speak*
*They said "Lord a plague is on the world*
*Lord no man is free*
*The temples that we built to you*
*Have tumbled into the sea*

94

*Lord, if you won't take care of us*
*Won't you please, please let us be"*
*And the Lord said*
*And the Lord said*

*I burn down your cities – how blind you must be*
*I take from you your children and you say how blessed*
*are we*
*You all must be crazy to put your faith in me*
*That's why I love mankind*
*Your really need me*
*That's why I love mankind*

Pretty typical Randy. Sarcastic. Sardonic. And right on the money.

My attorneys are drawing up the emailing contract. It turns out that there will be privacy surcharges and some severe penalties if prompt payment is not received. I don't recall the details but I think it has something to do with your firstborn.

Howie


*Hi Howie:*

*A man would have to do something rather strange to act as happy as my dogs do when I come home. My male dog jumps up and down. I would have some questions about a man who did that. I really gave this guy a chance. This is the third time I am seeing him. I tried. I know he is nice (probably has a rap sheet of crimes with the FBI) but at this stage of life I think that being able to talk, getting along peacefully on a daily basis, and enjoying each others company is more important than anything. Probably always was more important than anything but hormones rule when we are younger. Yes I do have to be physically attracted to the person but sometimes that comes through a turn on to their personality before the physical. Or maybe they are one and the same? Okay, I want the whole package, brains and to be attracted to whatever it is that attracts me. Pretty much what you said in your profile brains and laughter. This guy never smiles let alone talks.*

*Today is "get aggravated by my mother" day. I have to take her food shopping, put her meds in her little meds holder (all 25 of them) and take whatever abuse she feels necessary to hand out today. She blew me away yesterday with the story she had to tell me. Title... POSSESSED ALARM CLOCK Chapter One: She said that she woke up in the middle of the night and heard a very, very loud ringing. She looked around the room to see what electrical appliance might be making that noise. She said it was her alarm clock. She pushed every button on the alarm clock and it wouldn't stop. She unplugged it and it finally stopped. She put it under her bed (why?) and then it started to ring again. She decided it had a battery back up in it. Chapter Two.. The next morning her neighbor said to her....Did you hear the fire alarm last night? The whole second floor was out in the hall. My mother said....I didn't say a word. I said....about what (having already decided that it was the fire alarm not her funky clock) She said...I didn't want them to know that I woke up the whole floor.*

*I love some of the lines of the song. I particularly enjoyed that part where he addresses the fact that god doesn't give a crap about us. If there is a god I am positive he does not address each of our problems............I think right now this god has decided he made a great mistake and has decided to kill us all and start over as he well should! How could a god create such stupid creatures? Creatures that do not improve over the centuries but repeat the same behavior over and over and over?????? but with better electronics.*

*Boldness...........On a lighter note....are we going to meet in town for lunch or dinner or coffee or tea any time soon or do you have to get permission from your wife? The last few men I have met have been involved. One admitted it right away and the other took a few months.?????????????? and the madness goes on.   :-) One of them is a Phila. judge.*

*Phyl*


Miss P –

Happy "Get Aggravated at Mama Day" even though it turns out that you celebrated a little early.

When you ask if I need to get permission from my wife, are you asking about my ex-wife, my current wife, my common-law wife, the woman I'm engaged to, my Russian mistress, the woman I'm living with or someone I might have wed in Reno during a drunken, yet forgotten, binge? If you want a specific answer, you'll need to ask a less general question.

So here's what I think we should do. I'll give you my phone number (if a woman answers, just lower your voice and tell her that you're the guy who's coming to pick up the piano) and we can, by mutual agreement, find a suitable time and place to get together.

On second thought, don't say anything about picking up the piano. It would be a dead giveaway because I don't have one. Instead, just say that you're my proctologist and you need to talk to me about something personal.

Howie

**Note:**

The Randy Newman concert that I referred to was the first official date that Debbie and I went on. In pretty rapid succession, she and I went to a concert that my son played in a Philadelphia club (the audience loved the show; Debbie not so much), an Obama rally with some up and coming singer named Bruce Springsteen and a Delaware University football game (another event that didn't rank high on Debbie's list of fave's).

By then, it was clear that Debbie and I were moving in a very positive direction and it certainly became apparent that it was time for me to stop communicating with other women.

I don't remember how I explained that to Phyllis. I don't even remember if Phyllis and I even met. But I know for certain that, despite the more than pleasurable email exchanges, our relationship went no further.

# Tiffany

**Note:**

This sequence begins in the middle. It ends in roughly the same place. Much of the email exchange with Tiffany is missing but, as you will soon see, a lot has been saved.

Tiffany and I were best when writing, pretty much OK when talking on the phone and simply awful when together. Since most good relationships require being in the same room at least some of the time, Tiffany and I were less than ideally suited.

Nevertheless some of our emails seem sufficiently amusing to be included here.

The first one that hasn't been lost, misplaced or mutilated is from Tiffany. At this point we were well into an exchange. Apparently in my last communication I had whined about a visit with friends who had tragically provided sheets of less than 600 count fine Egyptian cotton.

This is where the story picks up:

*Howdie Howie, (How easy to slip to the silly side.)*

*Rough hearing about your nocturnal discomfort on hemp-like linens...guess you must have developed great stamina for the hardships of this veil of intermittent tears? All the better to take in the true experiences of others, I say.*

*Do you live downtown? I was in Philly on July 4, 1976. Wonderful day! I will be there in early October for a landscape conference. Maybe, just maybe, by then we might want to check out the lay of the land, so to speak. And maybe, just maybe, we could meet by a bend in the Schuylkill.*

*Do you feel at home in both CA and in PA? Where do you spend more of your time?*

*Tiffany*


Hi Tiffany (sorry – it's not as silly or clever an opening as yours)

Thanks for understanding and appreciating the depths of discomfort to which I am willing to succumb. I might also point out that not only did I spend the entire night on those barely humane sheets but, in the morning, as a truly noble act, I made no mention of the pitiful linen quality to my hosts.

We had a very near miss. In recent months my emails have been filled with important messages from people who seem to know me very well. They offer all sorts of solutions for my staying power, means of increasing my size, links to videos of famous people in compromised positions, access to inexpensive medications, solutions to all of my sexual problems and surefire ways to make an unnamed "her" squeal with delight. Sadly, due to my very busy schedule, I have not set aside sufficient time to read all of those messages and, instead, delete them almost as fast as they arrive. Because I had no idea what "rechauffe" meant (it was on the subject line of your email) I placed yours in the delete bin as well. But, before relegating it to the "totally, completely, gone forever" bin, I checked more closely and found that you had provided lots of valuable information but offered nothing even remotely X, XX or XXX rated. Fortunately, there are still plenty of others who seem to have that zone well covered.


In addition to meandering about America in search of America, there are some specific events that I want to attend. There is an accordion festival, a juggling festival and

100

several others of equally assured humor. Often, just after Halloween, I attend Punkin' Chunkin' - an absolutely absurd event that takes place in downstate Delaware. All sorts of contraptions have been devised to hurl, throw, shoot or otherwise launch pumpkins. Not surprisingly, there is a lot of silliness but there are some who take this very seriously. Air cannons with barrels that seem to be 75 feet long have shot pumpkins nearly a full mile – even though no explosives are permitted. And, on many occasions, some of the devices end up sending the pumpkins backwards and into the crowd. There has been great concern of late because the farmer who allows the Chunkers to use his field every year has now sold out to developers. It's even possible that the event may be moved to Maryland – and as you can surely understand, this would be a monumental and tragic loss to the state of Delaware.

Howie


*Howie,*

*Oh dear. You probably didn't realize how it works. All of those alluring e-ads are just fronts. Using the well-proven marketing device, "sex-sells," smart marketers have imbedded, for those willing to delve, a trove of real/useful information inside each email. For example, after reading testimonials about the successful use of ion strips to recharge your carnal energy, there are instructions for building the most powerful trebuchet ever to heave a pumpkin! Can you imagine! So sorry you missed a possible championship.*

*The conference I am attending offers a slew of field trips and I was not sure just what I'd enjoy most. I ended up selecting a trip to the Morris Arboretum and a few local grand gardens ---but am second-guessing my choice. Have you ever been to Chanticleer?*

*Tif*

Miss T –

Thanks for the tip on the secret instructions hidden in the bowels of otherwise suspect emails. Now, knowing the depths of their importance, I will forward them all to you – along with the phone number of several physicians you might call if you should incur a 4-hour erection. If I had one, I wouldn't call a doctor, I'd call everyone I know. But I suspect that your personal reactions might be somewhat different: in addition to abject concern, there would probably be overwhelming confusion.

I've never heard of the Coney Island Mermaid parade but I do know about – and have attended – the Doo Dah parade in Pasadena. It takes place at the end of December one week before the Rose Bowl parade. The rules for participating are pretty simple – if you wanna be in, you're in. The Bridge to Breakers parade in San Francisco is also pretty much of a hoot. It's not surprising that a few thousand gays dressed up and ready to party can form the substance of some remarkable frivolity.

It's way too early for me to even get a feel for Philadelphia. I've walked the city – at least the downtown sections – but really don't know it at all. Sadly, I am unable to offer suggestions about what to see and what to avoid during your autumnal visit.

For numerous reasons – all of them good – it feels to me that it's time to kick this up a notch. Are you ready for the next step in communicating? I'll be happy to call you if you let me know your phone number. But, if you'd rather be the one to push the buttons, here's mine: 000-000-0000.

Mr. Howie


**Note:** At this point there is a break in the email activity probably, although not certainly, due to some telephonic communication.

The gist of what is missing is a planned get-together at a place that is acceptably inconvenient to both of us.

The next email is from me:

So Miss T –

We're on for Thursday evening.
6 o'clock at the Hamilton Grill Room

Try not to wear something diffident, dissident or different.
Ravishing would be good. Ravished would be bad.
I, however, will be in jeans.

Howie

*Sir,*

*Thanks a bunch, as they say in the upper western regions of these our dissonant states...for the encouragement and the reservation. I will be wearing my new garden smock, daisy-print apron and pink sun-visor. Hopefully I will be able to find enough naphtha soap to suppress the fertilizer aroma and lighten my nails.*

*TR*

*P.S. Are you one of those one-name monikered people like Che or Cher?*


Miss T –

Wardrobe is such a worry. I've found that it's hard to go wrong with basic black, pearls and gloves. But that's me. You, of course, are welcome to your own fashion standards. You will, however, be judged.

My last name is Krakow. The city in Poland (where the last pope was from) was named in my honor although the naming was several thousand years before my actual birth. But those Poles...somehow they always knew. And you needn't be concerned about addressing me as Mr. Krakow. We know each other well enough that a simple, "your lordship" will suffice.

Howie

**Note:**

We met. We dined. We talked. We did not, however, bond.

Attempting to pinpoint why there was no magic is a waste of energy. Sometimes meshing is inevitable, if unexplainable. More often, though, the chemistry fails to ignite.

Although we had a lot in common, what we didn't have in common was each other. What should have been easy conversation turned out to be strained. What was anticipated as a light, enjoyable evening turned out to be heavy and uncomfortable.

Somehow, during the course of the evening, it was revealed that in my Profile, I had fudged my age by a few years. For her, that horrific realization was terminal. The depth of my deceit signaled a life built on lies and dishonesty.

It wasn't an awful meeting. But it was much less than promising. For both of us, it was a letdown.

And, though the emails continued and there were attempts at amusing banter, the trajectory definitely pointed in a negative direction.


Mine was first:

Miss T –

Whew. I'm glad that the first uncomfortable episode is now history and, hopefully, you are feeling at least a little less pressured. If you felt that I was expecting too much, too soon, you should be relieved to know that I have cancelled both the banquet hall for the wedding reception as well as the caterer. Nevertheless, I think it's only fair that you come up with your 50% of the cancellation fee especially given that you were the one who, if memory serves me correctly, demanded the all-vegetarian, non-dairy, smoke-free faux pork sausage with ham hocks and kidney beans menu.

As you continue to juggle new business, old business, existing business and a move into a new home and office, I might be able to help. Not only am I a marketing consultant but, based on no experience and even less knowledge, I can offer - at no cost or obligation - my time management advice.

It appears that you need to multi-task. So here are a few surefire ways:

1. Even though you have not told me so, I would surmise that you are not accomplishing very much when you sleep. Those hours, while valuable in a recuperative sense should not be wasted and could be used to do so much more. For example, why not combine eating and sleeping? Emailing when asleep makes a great deal of sense. Not only can the recipient read the mail at a later, more appropriate time but you can be forgiven for any fuzzy thinking by offering the excuse "Sorry, I wasn't really awake when I wrote that."

2. It seems to me that you are spending a lot of time driving around. Not only is that expensive - especially given the high cost of gas - but it is also inefficient. Here's an obvious solution: simply suggest to your current and new clients that they all move to the same location. Not only will that make your scheduling easier but, if you can also convince them to occupy the same type of housing, you could provide them all with precisely the same design.

3. Help. Although Russo Intergalactic Landscape Design Inc. is obviously a giant corporation; it appears that the staff is rather limited. That's understandable given the normal expense of salaries, benefits, insurance and taxes. But there is an easy way around that. Why not consider

indentured servants? Oh sure, there are a few outdated covenants that might call into question some legal issues but with a little effort you should be able to find some sleazy attorney who can keep your servants wallowing fruitlessly in the court system for years. As a practical suggestion, if they throw the book at you, simply take the most propitious route and just duck.

4. The first 3 suggestions are free. But I can assure you that there are many more - equally brilliant - ideas yet to come, all at a price to be negotiated.


As you have undoubtedly determined, today's plate is less filled for me than it is for you. But I can assure you that, even given a full load, I can almost always find time for frivolity.

Howie


*Hi Howie,*

*Thanks for the excellent advice; I will try very, very hard to institute all of your suggestions.Today is my birthday, a useful point for making changes.*

*I don't have create-a fun-and-games note kinda time right now, but wanted to say hi as I head out the door to find some nice birthday cake to take to my landlady's friend for dinner....landlady is in LA but friend is recuperating from liposuction and making me dinner as my sister had to cancel. Oh those stories, oh , those lives.......*

*TR*

Miss T –

Because I knew your birthday was last week but was unsure of the precise date I decided to send huge flower bouquets every day. I probably shouldn't tell you, but in the interest of total transparency, I did get a heck of a deal from the mortuary. Apparently the bereaved family was a little overzealous about the guy's death. The way it was explained to me, he did not pass away but had, in actuality, passed gas. Hopefully you were not too upset about the "Sorry for your Loss" message spelled out in carnations and crepe paper but, as they say, it's the thought that counts.

No doubt you understood that the generous array of birthday cards and gifts that others offered were, in fact, all from me. It's just my way of spreading kindness along with birthday salutations. Please don't tell your friends and relatives that you know the true giver – it would make them feel cheap, tawdry and might have a serious impact on my close, personal relationship with all of them.

Now that you have celebrated a birthday, it makes you closer to my reported – albeit inaccurate – Match.com Profile age. I am now in the process of changing it. I'm thinking 36-39. Having actually met me in person, you may feel that shaving several decades might be somewhat of a stretch but by offering a range I feel that I'm making allowances for interpretation. Another thought was to list my age as 50 plus or minus 25.

Will your meeting in Philadelphia be held at the Pennsylvania Horticultural Society? I've been walking by their offices since I moved here because the building is about 2 blocks from my house. The word "horticulture" always makes me smile. Although I know there's a good line waiting to be written, I've never been able to come up with the ending to, "you can lead a whore to culture but...."

By the nature of this email you might surmise that I have

too much time on my hands and a surplus of silliness that is difficult to curtail – kind of like the way things were in my 9th grade English class where I always seemed to be in trouble for being somewhat off message.

But there is a difference. In 9th grade, I was unable to stop. But now, as a mature 36-39 year-old, I can.

See.

Howie

*Howie,*

*Ah, but I was aware of the origin of the hearse-load of flowers as the banners said "Made in Poland." Reminds me of the joke about the...I forgot the rest. I appreciated the permanence of the flowers and the brightness of the colors, especially the turquoise lilies with the extra-large glitter. Thank you.*
*The conference I am attending is for the American Society of Landscape Architects. I'm not staying in town (a penny-pinching decision) -- rather, staying with a friend in NJ just over the border in Frenchtown. This does mean that I will be driving back and forth more than I would like and keeping me from any free time. Maybe we can chat by phone about getting together.*

*Tif*

Miss T –

How is it that, at the stroke of Sept. 22, the weather changes and summer disappears in a flash? Today is dark and almost blustery. Time to start packing for Southern California.

Here's a suggestion – something that I would rather offer and have you reject than not offer at all under the premise that you'd probably reject it.

First, a quick geography lesson: Frenchtown is about as convenient to Philadelphia as it is to Manhattan. It's at least an hour away. That means, every day you're at the conference you'll be spending at least 2 hours on the road. I do, however, understand why, from a financial standpoint, that's preferable to a more convenient, albeit more expensive, hotel.

So here's my suggestion: consider staying at my place. Although my apartment is hardly huge, it does have a guest room. To give you an indication of the privacy it provides, that room has been occupied by a friend from California. She is married to another good friend who I've known for a very long time so, if the accommodations weren't reasonable, all of us would feel uncomfortable about the arrangement.
If you are concerned about my expectations, please put your mind to rest. You don't have to carve out time for me. You don't have to worry about your bones being jumped. I'm just talking about a private room in an apartment that's about an hour closer to the only reason you're in Philadelphia.

Howie

*Hey.Howie –*

*...nice offer! I have still not settled my lodging arrangement--and was concerned about the daily trek. It does seem a little crazy for me to stay at your place because, as Geraldine used to say, "You don't KNOW me!" And vice versa. But it would certainly be very nice for me! Aren't you going to be away a portion of the weekend anyway?*

*How's about we chat on the phone about it. Are you home today?*

*Tif*

**Note:** At this point there is a pause in the written exchange.

It's possible that some emails have been lost. It's more likely that there were phone conversations. The topic was almost certainly about Tiffany's upcoming visit to Philadelphia.

The recovered emails resume with this one from her:

*H –*

*L'shana tova!*

*I hope you are celebrating a new beginning in these hard times with thoughts of affluence...or at least an affluence of thoughts. What DO the American people want!!??*

*I was just looking over my outgoing mail and do not see a note to you about the parking arrangement. I wrote it...must have closed my email without sending. Seemingly rude, I will call you today. Is there a good time?*

*Tif*

Miss T –

I'm not celebrating with thoughts of affluence – only flatulence. It appears that for "non-political" reasons, Congress just shit on the country.

Call anytime.

I just checked in the neighborhood and found an indoor garage that is about 2 minutes from my apartment. The cost for parking you car there – from Thursday afternoon until Tuesday will be about $60. That's if you leave it there the whole time - without in and out privileges. You really shouldn't need your car while you're here - the convention center is less than a 10-minute walk from my place.

If you decide to take Amtrak to Philadelphia, the 30th street station (it's the main train terminal) is about a 15 minute walk from my apartment.

So, factor in convenience, the cost of gas and anything else and make your decision.

I'm assuming that you're coming on Thursday - is that right? Any idea what time? I don't need an accurate ETA - but a general indication would be helpful. I want to make sure    the    marching    band    is    ready.

Howie

**Note:**

Tiffany came to Philadelphia for the Landscape Conference and stayed at my apartment for a few days. As far as a potential relationship between the two of us, to the surprise of neither, it was a completely uneventful visit.

Although parking seemed to have been a major concern, she was able to find a space on the street and save the $60 garage fee. That was the good news about her car. The bad news – and the last I heard from her – was that on the way to Chanticleer Gardens, she had an accident. She was fine. The car was not.

For reasons that are still unclear to me even now, I thought that was a fitting way to conclude the Tiffany chapter of my life.

# It started with a number.

One of my earliest exchanges was with a woman who turned out to be writing a book about online dating (obviously a concept that will never work). This was in the very early days of meeting online when there were few dating sites and the ones that did exist were still trying to figure out how to make it work.

Later on the process got very organized. There were detailed Profile outlines to help you to describe yourself and your hoped-for mate. There were memberships, monthly fees and lots of communication along with helpful recommendations from the sites about what to say and how to say it. But in the beginning, everything was much more freewheeling. There were few restrictions. As long as you were willing to pay by the word, you could write whatever you wanted. Essentially you posted an ad and sometimes a photo. In this particular instance, although the ad was almost certainly interesting, the photo was more than sufficient to merit a response.

This is how the exchange began:

Dear 2117 –

So, are the emails coming through in droves?  They ought to - your photo looks great, you seem interested in just about everything, you've done a lot and still remain surprisingly optimistic, and geographically, you're within range of a mere 8 million people.

There's a lot on your wish list, but you're offering a lot, too. So...

For the record, this is a partial indication of who I am. I'm 5' 8", relatively fit, have a Masters Degree, and am both single and divorced. (Amazingly, I am capable of both simultaneously).  I have two sons, 24 and 26. Both of them are significantly more mature than their father. I'm 56 (but can easily pass for 55 1/2).

Other pertinent but not necessarily valuable information: for about 20 years I lived in Hollywood and did the Hollywood thing. I wrote screenplays, sitcoms, and produced TV shows. The money was good; the sense of self-satisfaction ...not so much. All of the oft-mentioned stereotypes applied: too much ego and too little substance. So about 8 years ago I discarded all pretense, packed my bags, moved to New York and re-entered the questionably ethical world of advertising as a partner in one of New York's most successful agencies. Then, a little over a year ago, at the stroke of the millennium, I decided it was time to either kick back completely or take my shot at the pot of gold at the end of the dotcom rainbow.

I chose door number 2. But it seems that someone moved the particular pot I was attempting to confiscate. So, I took some time off, although I continued to consult with a few companies that, with my valuable assistance, managed to shut down completely in near record time.

I'll be glad to supply more information, more facts, or more non-sequiturs upon request. If names are important to you, I have one. Most people call me Howie. And, when they do, I usually respond.

The photo is pretty accurate. I tend to squint when I laugh - and I try to laugh as much as possible.  But, in case you're concerned, I do have eyes (they're kinda green).

I look forward to hearing from you - if only to let me know that the email got through.

Howie

*Hi Howie,*

*Sure your email got thru. Photo too. Thanks!*

*To be honest, yes, the emails are coming in droves. Of course, it doesn't hurt to have 2 ads up in different locations. Then there's the problem of the getting hit on from all sides by the same ... er, Respondents.*

*And to be really honest, I recently started seeing someone (he's 57 yrs old, 25 miles away). I'm a serially monogamous dater so I don't think I'll be juggling.*

*However, I'm always up for email pals. If you're still interested, feel free to write back. I would be very interested in hearing more of your adventures/stories. I'd love to hear about your adventures in Hollywood and Dot-com casualties. Details are always good, including vital stats such as:*

*Your exact birth date (time of day & location scores big points!)*

*Your current occupation, net income, religion, likes/dislikes Any irritating personal habits, dreams, fantasies, reference from your therapist, weird dating habits, HIV status, mother's maiden name, favorite fruit (no, not Richard Simmons), license plate#, police record, last book read, college GPA, geographic location, batting average, shoe size, favorite color, and date of last oil change.*

*I probably don't have to caution you to avoid clichés such as "I like walking on moonlit beaches holding hands" - lest I throw up.*

*Just keep in mind that you're on the "agency" side - while I sell print space for a living ... to be COMPLETELY honest!*

*Dorothy*

Hi Dorothy,

Thanks for answering.

Can't say I'm surprised to hear that you're being inundated by emails or that you're now in the early stages of a new relationship - even if the lucky guy does happen to live 25 miles away.

Like you, I'm a fan of monogamy. I don't think of dating as an activity; it's more like a pursuit. You do it until you find someone you like enough to STOP dating.

And, like you, I'm always up for worthwhile correspondence.

With all of that similar thinking as a base, I was truly amazed to hear that you still want honesty from a guy. Perhaps over the years, you've noticed that it's not something we of the male persuasion tend to do very well.

I'd love to be able to say that I, alone amongst men, am consistently truthful. I could say that, but my nose would grow. Actually, I'm pretty good about not lying - mainly because I find that it's very difficult to keep track of past fabrications in current conversations. But, I certainly have strayed into the "guilt by omission" territory. I think that's fairly typical. Women say everything: what they want, what they like, what they feel. Men tend to say...well, nothing. I guess our theory is that by not saying anything, at least we haven't told any lies. I'm not saying it's a good theory. I'm not saying I'm proud to be a subscriber. But I do think that at least being conscious of the problem offers some hope of solving it.

So, following that line of thinking, here are some honest answers IN ALL CAPS to your many and varied questions. Hollywood tales and specifics of internet incompetence will be cheerfully provided later, if you're still interested.

Your exact birth date (time of day & location scores big points!)

APRIL 11, 1942. 5 A.M. THE BRONX. (DATE AND LOCATION ARE CERTAINLY CORRECT. THE EXACT TIME IS ANYBODY'S GUESS.)

Your current occupation, net income, religion, likes/dislikes

CURRENTLY RETIRED FROM THE 9-5 WORLD, BUT ACTIVE TO A DEGREE THROUGH CONTINUING CONSULTING PROJECTS (MARKETING, BUSINESS-BUILDING AND ENTERTAINMENT). I'M A BIT DISQUIETED BY THE THOUGHT OF REVEALING NET INCOME, BUT SUFFICE IT TO SAY THAT I'M ABLE TO MAINTAIN THE SAME LIFESTYLE I HAD WHEN I WAS ONE OF 20 PARTNERS IN AN AD AGENCY THAT BILLED $1.5 BILLION AND HAD ABOUT 700 EMPLOYEES. (IN OTHER WORDS, I CAN AFFORD TO GO TO DINNER EVEN IF IT'S AFTER THE CUT-OFF TIME FOR EARLY-BIRD SPECIALS).

MY PARENTS WERE BOTH JEWISH, SO TECHNICALLY I AM AS WELL. BUT IN ACTUALITY, I'M AN AVID NON-PRACTICER OF ANY FORMAL RELIGION. I'M BIG ON ETHICS, RESPONSIBILITY AND FAIRNESS. BUT GOD AND I DON'T TALK MUCH. EVEN IN SACRED HOUSES OF WORSHIP WE EACH ACT AS IF THE OTHER DOESN'T EXIST.

LIKES AND DISLIKES? I LIKE POWERFUL, SMART, ARTICULATE PEOPLE WHO HAVE INFORMATION TO SHARE. I LIKE PEOPLE WHO HAVE STRONG PREFERENCES - EVEN IF THEY SHARPLY DISAGREE WITH MY OWN BELIEFS. (I'D RATHER BE IN SOMEONE'S TERRIBLY DECORATED HOME THAN ONE THAT WAS CONVENTIONALLY DONE BY A DECORATOR). I'M A BIG FAN OF NON-CONFORMITY, ESPECIALLY IF THE POSITION TAKEN IS DUSTED WITH AT LEAST A BIT OF AMUSEMENT. I LIKE A LOT MORE - BUT THAT'S ENOUGH POSITIVE STUFF FOR NOW BECAUSE I ALSO HAVE A STRONG CURMUDGEON SIDE.

I DON'T LIKE THE BEACH - MOONLIT OR OTHERWISE. I
DON'T LIKE THE FEEL OF SAND BETWEEN MY TOES OR IN
MY BED. I DON'T LIKE THE TASTE OF SALT WATER. I
DON'T LIKE SOGGY SHEETS. I DON'T LIKE BEING
SUNBURNED. I DON'T LIKE CARRYING A LOT OF
PARAPHENALIA (COOLERS, UMBRELLAS, CHAIRS,
SUNSCREEN, TOWELS, ETC.). I DON'T LIKE LATHERING UP
WITH SUNSCREEN BUT FEAR THE SUN'S POWER EVEN
MORE. I DON'T LIKE BEING OUT IN THE OPEN AND BEING
CROWDED BY LOUD PEOPLE WHOSE BLOATED BODIES ARE
IMPERFECT FITS FOR THEIR SKIMPY BATHING SUITS.
AND, HAVING SAID ALL THAT, I RENTED A HOUSE ON FIRE
ISLAND LAST JULY AND ENJOYED EVERY MINUTE I SPENT
THERE.

I DON'T LIKE THE PEOPLE WHO TALK TOO LOUDLY IN
RESTUARANTS AND LAUGH AT HIGH VOLUME UNLESS THEY
HAPPEN TO BE SITTING AT MY TABLE (IN WHICH CASE THE
BOISTROUS HILARITY IS TOTALLY APPROPRIATE). I DON'T
LIKE PEOPLE WHO ARE AFRAID TO SPEAK THEIR MIND. I
DON'T LIKE PEOPLE WHO AGREE WITH WHAT I'M SAYING
BEFORE I FINISH SAYING IT. I DON'T LIKE THE FACT THAT
WHEN I TRAVEL, I'M OFTEN INTIMIDATED BECAUSE I
DON'T SPEAK THE NATIVE LANGUAGE.

Any irritating personal habits, dreams, fantasies, reference
from your therapist, weird dating habits, HIV status,
mother's maiden name, favorite fruit (no, not Richard
Simmons), license plate#, police record, last book read,
college GPA, geographic location, batting average, shoe
size, favorite color, and date of last oil change.

IRRITATING HABITS? WHILE NOT TECHNICALLY A
NEATNESS FREAK, I DO TEND TO LEAN IN THAT
DIRECTION. I'M OFTEN TOO QUICK TO TURN OFF THE
LIGHTS, PUT THINGS AWAY AND BECOME FRUSTRATED BY
PEOPLE WHO ARE NOT CONSCIENTIOUS ABOUT ARRIVING
ON TIME. OTHER THAN THAT, I THINK IT'S SAFE TO SAY
THAT I'M ABSOLUTELY WITHOUT FAULT. OH, AND ON

OCCASION, I DO LIKE TO DRESS SMALL DOGS IN BLACK NEGLIGE AND TALK DIRTY TO THEM. (IS THAT SO WRONG?).

DREAMS? A WEAK AREA FOR ME. I KNOW I DREAM BECAUSE I KNOW THAT EVERYONE DOES. BUT I DON'T REMEMBER MINE. IN FACT I'M SO GOOD AT NOT REMEMBERING THAT I FEEL AS IF I DON'T DREAM AT ALL.

FANTASIES? AGAIN A WEAK AREA. I'M VERY MUCH A REALIST AND A PRAGMATIST. I'M PRACTICAL TO A FAULT. THAT DOESN'T MEAN I'M NOT UP FOR ADVENTURE OR DOING NEW THINGS. I HOPE IT DOESN'T MEAN I'M BORING (I'D HATE KNOWING ANYONE THOUGHT THAT ABOUT ME). MAYBE IT'S A MATTER OF DEFINITION. I THINK OF FANATASY AS SOMETHING THAT COULD NEVER HAPPEN. WHAT I ENVISION ARE THINGS THAT I'D LKE TO DO AND THEN I TRY TO FIGURE OUT HOW TO ACCOMPLISH THEM.

THERAPIST'S REFERENCE. "HOWIE IS MUCH BETTER NOW. BUT I STILL RECOMMEND KEEPING HIM AWAY FROM SHARP OBJECTS, HOT LIQUIDS, AND EXPLOSIVES."

WEIRD DATING HABITS? OF COURSE, FEW MEN THINK OF THEMSELVES AS WEIRD. BUT FOR SOME STRANGE REASON, OTHERS DON'T NECESSARILY SHARE THAT OPINION - EVEN IN MY CASE. HERE IS SOMETHING THAT I KNOW IS A LONG WAY FROM PERFECTION. I TEND TO BECOME INVOLVED IN RELATIONSHIPS RATHER QUICKY. AND I TEND TO END THEM QUICKLY, TOO. THERE ARE UNDOUBTEDLY VALID REASONS FOR MY DESIRE TO EXIT, BUT THE FACT REMAINS THAT SOMEHOW, FOR ME, 4 MONTHS SEEMS TO BE THE TIME WHEN I SAY GOODBYE. IF IT ONLY HAPPENED ONCE, THERE WOULD BE NOTHING TO QUESTION. THE FACT THAT IT'S HAPPENED A HALF DOZEN TIMES DOES INDICATE A ISSUE. MAYBE I JUMP IN TOO SOON. MAYBE I PICK THE WRONG PEOPLE. OR MAYBE - DIFFICULT AS THIS MAY BE TO BELIEVE - I'M THE

PROBLEM. I REALLY DON'T BELIEVE THAT I'M COMMITTMENT-PHOBIC, THOUGH HISTORY INDICATES OTHERWISE. I GUESS THAT QUALIFIES AS WEIRD. IT CERTAINLY QUALIFIES AS "HONEST".

HIV STATUS? FINALLY A QUESTION THAT I CAN ANSWER WITH THE ASSURANCE THAT I'M SAYING NOT ONLY WHAT IS TRUTHFUL BUT ALSO WHAT IS PREFERRED. I'VE PASSED EVERY TEST. NO ISSUE HERE.

MOTHER'S MAIDEN NAME: GOLDSTEIN. (THERE'S A LOT MORE I COULD OFFER ABOUT HER - BUT THAT'S FOR ANOTHER TIME).

FAVORITE FRUIT. THE OBVIOUS QUALIFIER HERE IS THAT, WITH FRUIT, THERE'S A FRESHNESS FACTOR THAT MUST BE CONSIDERED. PICKED AT THE RIGHT TIME, ALMOST ANY FRUIT CAN KNOCK ME ON MY ASS. GETTING OUT OF SEASON ANYTHING - EVEN A FAVORITE - AT THE GROCERY STORE OFTEN MEANS A MOUTHFUL OF MEALY NOTHING. SO, ASSUMING THAT WE'RE TALKING THE BEST OF THE FRESHEST, I'M GOING WITH PINEAPPLE. A RIPE, SWEET/TART PINEAPPLE CAN BRING ME TO MY KNEES. I'M ALSO BIG ON CHERRIES - BLACK, YELLOW OR RED - AS LONG AS THEY'RE LARGE AND FIRM.

LICENSE PLATE NUMBER: I'M A MANHATTAN BOY. NO CAR. NO LICENSE NUMBER.

POLICE RECORD: ONLY CAUGHT ONCE: FOR PUBLIC INTOXICATION WHEN I WAS A COLLEGE SENIOR OVERINDULGING IN SPRING BREAK AT DAYTONA BEACH. I LEARNED MY LESSON. NOW I DON'T HANG AROUND WITH UNSAVORY PEOPLE, DON'T CARRY CONCEALED WEAPONS, AND DON'T SAY ANYTHING NEGATIVE ABOUT MEN WITH NICKNAMES THAT BEGIN WITH THE WORD "THE" (AS IN BENNY "THE EXECUTIONER").

LAST BOOK. I READ A LOT. LATELY I'VE BEEN DOING SHORT STORIES. LOTS OF MEDIOCRE WORK, BUT HERE ARE A FEW I LIKED: <u>FOR RELIEF OF UNBEARABLE URGES</u> BY NATHAN ENGLANDER. <u>CIRCLING THE DRAIN</u> BY AMANDA DAVIS. <u>NAKED PUEBLO</u> BY MARK JUDE POIRIER. THE LAST BOOK THAT MADE ME CRAZY BECAUSE I LIKED IT SO MUCH WAS <u>A HEARTBREAKING WORK OF STAGGERING GENIUS</u> BY DAVE EGGERS.

COLLEGE GPA: 3.5 AS AN UNDERGRADUATE. 3.6 IN GRAD SCHOOL. (ACTUALLY I DON'T REMEMBER EITHER ONE, BUT GIVE OR TAKE A HALF POINT OR SO, THESE ARE PROBABLY FAIRLY ACCURATE).

GEOGRAPHIC LOCATION: I HAVE A LOFT IN TRIBECA. I'M CURRENTLY LOOKING FOR A COUNTRY PLACE IN PA.

BATTING AVERAGE: I TEND TO HIT FOR POWER, SO MY AVERAGE ISN'T AS HIGH AS MIGHT BE DESIRED. I'M ALSO A PULL HITTER, SO THE OTHER TEAM OFTEN EMPLOYS A SHIFT - WHICH ALSO CUTS DOWN ON HITS. ACTUALLY I WISH I HAD A BATTING AVERAGE. IT'S BEEN WAY TOO LONG SINCE I PLAYED IN A LEAGUE. I WAS NEVER REALLY GOOD OR REALLY BAD. BUT I WAS ALWAYS THE ONE WITH THE BIGGEST MOUTH.

SHOE SIZE: ACTUALLY 10. BUT, FOR DATING PURPOSES, I LIKE TO SAY 11½.

FAVORITE COLOR: I HATE THAT THIS IS TRUE, BUT IT IS: GRAY. I LIVE MY LIFE IN ABSOLUTES - FOR ME THINGS ARE USUALLY EITHER BLACK OR WHITE. BUT SOMEHOW, GRAY WORKS WELL FOR ME. I FIND IT SOOTHING, I FIND IT BRINGS OUT THE COLOR IN EVERYTHING ELSE, AND AS A BACKGROUND COLOR IT'S A LOT MORE DYNAMIC THAN WHITE. THAT BEING SAID, I TEND TO DRESS IN A LOT OF BLUES AND GREENS.

LAST OIL CHANGE? NO CAR. NO LICENSE PLATE. NO OIL CHANGE.

HONEST ENOUGH FOR YOU?

Howie


*H –*

*Thanks for taking the time to complete the survey, and for giving me such detailed - and entertaining - information, Howie (love the comment on shoe size). It will go into your dossier. And thanks for the book leads - I've been meaning to read: "A Heartbreaking Work..." and your recommendation is a good reminder.*

*I can't comment on ALL your answers (I'm lazier than you are) but your "weird dating habits" comments do strike a chord. Then I noted your birthday (yeah - I'm one of those spacy chicks) and can tell you right away that, as an Aries male, you're right out of the books. (I'm March 28th B-Day, so I can testify.) Typical Arien behavior - early flash-point, quickly stalking the game -- leading to early burnout ... then, NEXT! It's a Good Thing you're at least aware of it, which is more than I can say for most. I've behaved in much the same manner most of my "dating" life. My last long-term relationship, Raymond (he's 13 years younger and we share a 12-yr old daughter) - tried to get my number at a McGee screenwriting seminar @ Hunter College (I took his) - a week later, he came over for dinner - and never left. Typical. So up until recently, I've been a Millennium Flower Child, but since moving up to God's country, and also reaching the age of "diminished expectations" (let's face that reality, shall we?) .. I've had to conform/behave like most people (well, most WOMEN) who date "sensibly". Oy. Not my nature.*

*I'm finding that so many of the people I've met online (including the Magistrate who I'm dating) are seriously scarred casualties in the War between the Sexes (including the scars from their moms & pops of course) that it's been difficult to retain my inherent sense of optimism and hope (fairy-tale delusional dust?). I'm also constantly thinking about that old saying "a cynic is a failed optimist/bitter romantic" (whatever it is, can't remember) being true - and that if opportunity presented itself, wouldn't we all shed that armor and jump in? This assumes we can actually recognize opportunity when it comes along.*

*I just opened an email with an opener along the lines of " Hi - Let's meet ...I'm between woman (sic)..." Now doesn't that just make you want to jump in?*

*Last night I finally had a phone conversation with a dude I've been emailing on/off for the past 3 years (he also lives about 25 miles away) and have never actually met. He's an ex-therapist, very cynical, definitely bitter and hysterically funny and exhilarating - and one of the conversation openers was him telling me how he's (well, aren't all guys?) a prisoner of his own dick and how he hates it and wishes he could do get rid of it. I made some comment about what transsexuals do... and he said if he could, he'd do it in an instant. (How many opening social conversations do you have that bring up castration?) And of course, this conversation went on for over 2 hours (on my dime!) and free-ranged and ranted all over the place. And I'm thinking .... HOW much do these guys charge an hour? Of course, I'm not the most focused of people, and he admits to having adult A.D.D... so the sidebars were coming fast & furious.*

*Back to being completely honest: I should warn you that I'm working on a book project with all of this and that's one of the reasons I'm interested in writing to you (and other intelligent life forms). If you'd like to share any of your war-stories, opinions etc., I'd be very interested. Names changed to protect the guilty and all that.*

*Where in Tribeca are you? I commute to NYC and work on Fifth & 16th St - although my company is on the block and may be sold over the summer. (Reminder - call that headhunter.)*

*Howie, I'm working from my home office in Orange county today and must do farm chores before I start hitting people up for advertising dollars. This includes hanging up 4 loads of wash, weeding some stuff, making fresh horseradish from the sink full of roots that the Magistrate had brought over the other night from his place, making some rhubarb coffee cake & sauce from the 50 dozen plants that have taken over my garden ... and then going for a walk around the "block" - in this case, a 4.2 mile route past the dairy farm, Pet cemetery, up to Route 17K and back down past the really old family plot at the beginning of my road where the guy who built most of this house (the new part is from 1840) and his wife are resting. I like to commune with them every so often and beg for help!*

*Thanks again and please write back anytime!*

*Dot*

Hi Dorothy -

Glad to hear that I made it through the survey with a passing mark. I was a little concerned because I was copying off some guy's paper, and he didn't seem confident about his answers. (I only copied on the multiple choice; I answered the essay questions all by myself).

If I provide nothing other than the impetus to read <u>A Heartbreaking Work...</u> this email exchange will have been worthwhile. Dave Eggers is young, but I think he's going to be an extremely important American writer - along the lines of Ken Kesey or Kurt Vonnegut. He has an effortless style but even more importantly, he seems to have a very sure understanding of popular culture. He's currently editing a quarterly journal that consistently offers some of the most inventive, off-beat and yet hysterically funny pieces that I've encountered of late. The works are of varying length, style, topic and importance. But even when I don't fully appreciate the quality, I'm always appreciative of the effort. I also notice that his name is beginning to be mentioned in ways that indicate he is having an impact far beyond his own writing and editing.

I'm not as quick to scoff at astrology as I once was. While I'm hardly willing to accept that all people born in a one-month period (all Aries, for example) are bound by certain character traits, I have found that when specifics (precise time and place of birth) are added into the equation, astrologers are able to offer some pretty fascinating information. I've had both good and bad experiences, but when the one guy got it right, he did spin my head around.

My last long-term relationship (a romance that lasted for several years and a friendship that has lasted considerably longer) was with a woman who's previous significant partner, like yours, was also 13 years younger. I think when they got together he was about 25. Clearly there's something very positive to be said about a young man who finds himself attracted to an older woman (older women?). She had nothing but wonderful things to say about him. She eventually broke off the relationship because she felt he was too young - not in terms of his maturity or in the way he treated her, but because he made her feel too matronly due to of his lack of worldly experiences. I always felt that kind of reasoning was akin to breaking up with a midget because he's too short.

The concept of older men with younger women is so readily accepted, but the reverse is seldom seen. My own feelings are that given all the difficulties of being a couple, if any two people - regardless of their ages, body types or personal hygiene - feel they've found a path to happiness, then we should just stand aside and applaud. In the past 5 years, my own failed relationships have been with women who ranged in age from 28 to 56. In many ways, they were all wonderful. There were many reasons why we didn't make an everlasting twosome, but age was never the determining factor.

I love that you're with a Magistrate. How does anyone compete with a title like that? Once, when I had a small company in L.A, we all chose our own titles. The youngest guy wanted to be Emperor. My partner wanted to be president. I became the Minister of Finance (figuring that the guy who held the purse strings would inevitably be the one that got sucked up to the most). Still, Magistrate beats them all.

The people you've met online are, I think, fairly typical of the people you'd meet anywhere. We're all scarred; especially those of us who think we got away clean. I'm finding that I'm more at ease with my craziness these days. Ever since I got away from the 12-hour days, the 6-day weeks, and the clients I felt were both arrogant and stupid, I've become a lot more tolerant. I find that I'm often amused by my own mellowness in the face of New York's constant abuse (visual pollution, obnoxious people or, as the heat increases, the astonishing aromas that waft above the garbage and through the streets).

While I understand your concern about the difficulty of maintaining a sense of cockeyed optimism as maturity and reality continue to smack us in the face, I'm nevertheless hanging on to the hope - however false it may be - that the best is yet to come. The alternative is acceptance, and I have too much fight left in me to give in yet. I have to admit, though, that I haven't opened as many emails as you, nor has anyone claimed to be "between men". Maybe it wasn't a typo or a grammatical mistake. Maybe he already had one and was hoping you'd join in a ménage a trois.

Even on your dime, the phone call to the ex-shrink sounds well worthwhile. Two hours of entertainment is hard to come by, and there's no question that you were entertained. I agree that any phone call that begins with a discussion about castration is, at the very least, unusual. Still, this guy sounds like someone best kept on the other end of a phone or a computer. 25 miles, in this case, might not offer you sufficient distance.

I think the idea that you're writing a book based on - or simply reprinting the emails - is terrific. I'll be glad to contribute war stories as they come to mind.

My apartment in on Warren Street, one block south of Chambers. I'm between West Broadway and Greenwich.

Tonight I was very close to your office. My oldest son, his girlfriend and I went to Barnes & Noble (the one just off of Union Square) to hear David Sedaris and another guy named David Something-or-Other read and sign books. If you don't know who David Sedaris is, we need to correct that immediately. He has a sense of humor that is simultaneously warped and right down the gut of what everyone is really thinking. The place was so jammed that they had to close off the floor 15 minutes early because there was no more room. Only in New York would a thousand people come to a bookstore to hear some guy read out loud. I was smiling before the reading began and continued laughing non-stop from then on. Definitely a fine evening.

Your list of morning chores frightened me. You accomplish more before you leave for the office than I manage to get done in an entire day. Maybe an entire week. And yours is the real stuff - the things that you can actually look at with a feeling of accomplishment (sort of the way I feel after I've done the dishes). Just a note: no one makes fresh horseradish. It comes in jars and you buy it at Zabars. I know because I just bought a jar of "extra strong". I have

128

no idea what to do with it, but I have wonderful memories of runny noses, tearing eyes, and a complete loss of my voice followed immediately by a sense of "wow, that was great!" Rhubarb is also one of my favorites - but I've yet to figure out how to make it so that it's neither too sweet nor too tart. I've missed badly and often on either end of the scale.

One more thing. Which is it: Dorothy or Dot? And how do you decide?

Howie

**Note:**

That's it. That's all. And whether her name is Dorothy or Dot will forever remain a mystery.

# Silly Snippets

Not every email exchange brimmed with information of consequence, humor or interest. While that may be a shocking revelation, it's important that some internet bubbles are burst sooner rather than later.

Although I was often pleasantly surprised by wit, charm or cleverness, there were plenty of times when I wasn't.

Many of the emails I received were entirely bereft of any potential whatsoever. Plucked from the exchanges that contained at least something worthwhile are these highly edited and incomplete bits and pieces.

# No Name

*You, sir, are a funny guy. You have your head on straight and your heart in line. I really liked all you had to say. And I hope maybe you'll say some more.....*

*I'm 47, 5'7", average build. I used to say I was a leggy blonde--like one would find on Baywatch but without the boobs. :) I have very little idea what I am today. I'm trying hard to get my head on straight and my heart in line after one of those hard to catch curve balls that life throws at you. (Don't care to talk about it--it's finally on the back burner and I want it to stay there.)*

*I could say I'm aggressively non-religious.*
*I have two degrees and am currently unemployed.*

*And I'm way over 5 miles from you--but then I'm interested in conversation........*

*What do you think?*


Dear over-educated and under-employed –

How many miles over 5 is "way over"?

OK, I have the Baywatch image firmly set in my mind. But, just to be sure you're the one I'm thinking of, are you the blonde who's running down the beach in slow motion? I hope you get there in time. You see, there's this big commotion...I'm not certain, but there seems to be something wrong in the ocean. Really. I'm not kidding. You better come quickly. Somebody could really, really get hurt. Maybe even drown or something, you know? But you're running so slowly...

That's when I woke up, so I don't know if you got there in time or if the kid (I'm assuming it was a kid) actually

131

drowned. I bet you'd feel real bad if he died...on account of how you weren't running fast and stuff.

OK. I feel a lot better now.

What was that photo/image/design that you sent? A checkerboard? A bent checkerboard? I got it, but I don't get it. Do you have a real photo? Preferably one taken on the beach in a day-glo orange bathing suit, holding a whistle, smiling and not looking at all like someone with 2 advanced degrees?

It's fine with me if you keep anything you want regarding head or heart alignment on the back burner, in the closet, or for that matter, filed away forever. But it is important that I know your hat size, least favorite vegetable and the number and expiration date of a valid credit card.

I guess I wasn't better after all.

Howie


**Note:**

I never heard from her again. But I can't say that was even remotely surprising.

# Bette

*Although a native Philadelphian, I'm actually not a big fan of the true Philly cheese steak (Velveeta...seriously??)*

*My trips to Ireland took me mainly from east to west in the traditional route - Dublin to Shannon through the southern counties. I'm a city girl at heart, so am in love with Dublin, but Ireland doesn't let you stay in one place for too long. Favorites are too many to count, but telling moments for me came at the Kilmainham jail (chilling); at the Old Head of Kinsale (extraordinary views of the mountains and sea -- and a great golf course); and at a tiny bar in Lisdoonvarna (Clare) that claims to be the last pub before New York (cheesy, but delightful). I don't think I'm quite finished with my travels there, so may yet get to see the country further north. And that concludes today's travelogue.*

*It's a sunny day, I'm at the beach, and so am off to perfect a wholly unhealthy tan. Just finished Predictably Irrational by Dan Ariely, so am looking for a new book. Any good recommendations?*

*Bette*

Hi Miss B –

Just so you're not confused about an issue of enormous importance...my understanding is that the cheese (or more correctly the "cheese food") of choice in the authentic Philadelphia cheese steak is not Velveeta but Whiz. If it's possible to make the very worst possible culinary decision, I think that Cheez Whiz would surely rank fairly high on the list. It would, however, fall somewhat beneath Spam, grits and another Pennsylvania favorite, scrapple. Like you, I am very much a city guy. Given a choice between the smells brought on by a freshwater stream flowing through a forest in autumn and a hot, humid day in

Manhattan where the aroma of dog urine wafts through the air, I'll take the canine smell every time. But Dublin, for some reason, didn't ring my bell. I was only there once and then only for a few days but I never quite got on the city's wavelength. That's possibly because I was always intimidated about driving on the wrong side of the road but if that excuse doesn't work, I'm sure I can come up with another.

I don't know Dan Ariely and never heard of Predictably Irrational so it's hard for me to offer a recommendation based on that information. Nevertheless, here's a thought:

Melissa Bank knocks me out. She writes connected short stories to create a novel. Her first book, The Girls Guide to Hunting and Fishing, was wonderful and her second (unnamed because my memory is total mush) is just as good.

Stay with the tanning concept. Sure it can lead to a painful, early death but at least you'll look healthy in the meantime.

Howie

**A**

*Your face looks so familiar I wonder if I actually wrote you at    some    other    point    in    time...odd....*

*Hey, before I went to med school, I was working in documentary films. Now I kind of want to be a botanist. Or maybe a large animal vet.*


Ms. A -

Would you prefer being a large animal vet or a veterinarian who treats large animals?  I think the decision will probably have an impact on your diet.

Howie

# Helen

*It's really old age. Forgive me. But I think you said we live too far apart ;or you weren't interested (both very good reasons). You just popped up on my screen again. If you have communicated the above to me, thanks for emailing me. I always think that is a nice gesture.*

*Good luck (again?) on your search.*

*Helen*


Hi Helen –

Must have been some other incredibly wealthy, talented, brilliant, handsome communicator.

What happened was...you winked at me (whatever that means) and I winked back (whatever that means).

I didn't write anything – nothing about being uninterested and nothing about living too far apart (although, to be honest, I have no idea where Montclair, NJ actually is).

But you're certainly welcome. I don't know precisely what you are welcome for but any time someone is willing to thank me, I try to be politely appreciative.

Howie

# Kandace

*Hi H:*

*My name is Kandace, I'm rich and healthy. Does that make you want to go steady. I loved that there is another out there that doesn't know what they want to be when they grow up. I am a perpetual toys' r' us kid. I'll never grow up.*

*I am also big on conversation. I am very smart and a real motor mouth. I also have a wicked sense of humor. So far so good. I do believe that laughter is food for the soul. I laugh a lot and love, love the sound of my own laughter. I know how to laugh at myself. I am a positive, upbeat, energetic, charismatic spiritual being having this human experience. Which means I'm not perfect, but almost. I, too am writing a book for the last ten years. It is called "Dancing in Walgreens."*

*I used to raise cockroaches, but I always need a challenge so now I'm raising a colony of ants who are prepared to do backflips at my signal.*

*So write already*

*Kandace*

Hi Ms. K -

I've never danced in Walgreens. In fact, since I left Chicago, I don't know if I've even been in a Walgreens. But, I understand your point: there's clearly something about that neon lighting from above and a set design consisting of 2300 various shades of pink fingernail polish that makes you want to slip into some dancing shoes and belt out a tune.

You may find that ants are a bit trickier than cockroaches. They come in droves, but then seem to disappear completely - probably at precisely the moment you want to show off their newly learned backflips. Roaches, on the other hand, NEVER go away. They just hide out until the light gets turned on and then, by their sheer girth and ugliness, scare the shit out of you. It's an old trick (about 2 billion years old, I understand) but it works every time.

Howie

## Gina

**Note:**

This exchange with Gina took place when the Seinfeld TV show was at the height of its success.


*H - You have a great sense of humor!!!!  I love it!!!!  I have a great idea for a sitcom... a show about nothing? :-)*

*G*


Miss G –

A show about nothing? Sure, it's a good idea, but it will never work. Too unconventional. Besides that kind of show would probably have to take place in NY, and the rest of America would never relate. I think we need a husband and wife, two cute kids (cut-ups, but in an adorable way), and maybe a screwball next-door neighbor. And the twist is...everyone is gay. Now that's high concept, don't ya think?

Howie

*G -*

*boy you're really smart!!!!  but...and there's always a but...I really like my idea and I have a good feeling about it. Maybe we should pitch it to someone nutty producer who eats in the wrong restaurants.   hmmm maybe the producer has this knockout gorgeous teenie bopper daughter and...*

*Gina*

Miss G –

You seem pretty committed to your concept, so I'm going to go along with you on this. Sometimes, it pays to just go with your gut.

Nevertheless, I'm afraid that it will be hard to find a producer with a beautiful teenage daughter. That would mean that the producer probably had a trophy wife - which would be an almost impossible find in Hollywood.

# Karen

*I am 57, and was widowed almost six years ago. I have a 21 year-old son who will be a senior in college (Wisconsin).I also have two step-children and a step-grandchild (is there such a thing?) in NYC.*

*Karen*


Karen –

When I was going to grad school in Chicago, I was quite familiar with the University of Wisconsin. At the time, it had the reputation for being the number 1 party school in the Midwest. My friends and I visited as often as possible - to help them maintain their hard-earned status. Now, I understand, it is better known for academics. What a shame.

I don't think there is such a thing as a step grandchild. All grandchildren are automatically granted full rights and status.

Howie

# Kelly

**Note:** Kelly was obviously doing some cutting and pasting for her responses and somehow used the name "Paul" in her note to me. I probably should have been offended but I was enjoying the process too much to be bothered about being addressed by another man's name.

*Hi Paul exaggerator,*

*Well, you really made me laugh. Are you as funny in person or by phone? I'm a Madonna twin, except that I'm not blond, I don't sing and I don't dance. I do travel both in the U.S. and Europe.*

*Do you really like Nina Simone, Dave Brubeck and live jazz? Well, I guess you can tell we're of the same era, except that I'mmuch younger than you.*

*By the way I actually saw Leon Redbone and he was terrific.*

*Kelly*

Hi Kelly -

No fair. I can't believe you went to see Leon Redbone without me. I found out that he was in town the day after he performed.

Am I as funny in person or by phone? I certainly hope so - but it depends a lot on the audience. If the people you're with give you nothing back, humor can be a lonely endeavor. Still...give me an inch, and I'll take an inch.

I guess there's no need for you to send a photo or describe yourself further - I've already seen plenty of Madonna pictures on TV and in the papers. I only hope that you're not as sexually repressed as she is.

Yes, I'd love to hear more about you. If you'd rather not send a photo, just refer me to the page of the Madonna book that is most representative of your current physique.

Howie

# Penny

*Dear Exaggerator,*

*You are adorable...silly man. I am clever, rich and .... yeah dream on. However, I have my talents, for instance I do speak Southern and have no trouble making myself understood in foreign countries...just talk louder.*

*Interested in your breeding stock. The only problem people have with roaches is they haven't gotten to really know them. How can you fault something that has been around for millions of years and can survive in the most hostile of conditions? How would you like to have to dodge a shoe sole every time some idiot decides to turn on a light.*

*I'm going to get my naturally (yeah) reddish hair tinted. Don't laugh just because you don't have to worry about yours.*

*Darn I knew the moon was full this weekend, what a terrible time. I even broke the toilet seat trying to stand on it. Pinches my butt every time I sit down....where's my duct tape. Later...*

*Hugs, Penny*


Miss P –

Here's something to remember: in the future, consider that the words "toilet seat" contain a clue as to proper use (the clue is in the "seat" part). Standing on them is not usually a good idea – regardless of the size or shape of the moon.

H

# Rachel

*Hi –*

*I'm 56, live in midtown.*

*My air conditioner isn't working so well. What else do strangers wonder about each other?*

*Rachel*

Rachel -

Fix the air conditioner fast. Or replace it. This is NY - you're not likely to get sympathy, so you might as well make yourself as comfortable as possible.

Howie

*Howie –*

*And...why is it I can't get any sympathy instead of an air conditioner?*

*Rachel*

Rachel –

Sympathy and air conditioners are both available. One comes with a financial price, the other an emotional one. On balance, air conditioners are a lot cheaper in the long run.

Howie

# No Name

**Note:**

This appears to be a random response from me. I have no recollection of why I wrote it or who the intended recipient was.

I'm afraid that your Miss Oxley has led you down the garden path. Her rule about "done" and "finished" is one that she personally conceived. It has no basis in the world of grammar. Certainly the word "done" is not limited to the completion of a baking task. I'm not sure where the precise line is drawn between the words done, finished, completed, ended, ready or through but I suspect that Miss Oxley should have stopped long before passing on misinformation to young and gullible minds. I don't know what her other rules might be but there is reason to believe that her decision to remain single was, quite possibly, not self-imposed.

# The Russian Connection

Initially the entry into the wonderful world of online dating begins with high hopes and positive expectations.

After all, there is at least an outside chance that Miss or Ms. Right actually does exist and will recognize wonderfulness, respond immediately and a life of assured fairy tale bliss will be enjoyed ever after.

While that may be a possibility, it soon becomes apparent that there is a surplus of Miss and Ms. Wrongs wandering the halls of cyberspace and they are doing their level best to escape.

Because the playing field turns out to be surprisingly large, the search process, though time consuming, is also invigorating. There is – not unhappily at first – a need to separate the wheat from the chaff. Sifting out those who don't make the cut for any number of blatantly obvious reasons is actually one of life's guilty pleasures. And unquestionably the opportunity to judge others as being inadequate is always a major boost to the ego. But the ego boost is short lived.

It doesn't take very long to realize that men and women seeking soul mates make up only a portion of the active online participants. Along with the innocent amateurs, there are hordes of professionals skillfully playing the game. While you may be an object of desire for some, for others you are nothing more than a target to be exploited.

There is an abundance of matchmaking services, porn sites, sexual enhancement products and sucker searchers prowling the web. Some are pretty clever. Others are less than subtle. None should be surprising. But, until the emails began to arrive with regularity, I was more of an innocent than I probably should have been.

Included here are a few that are pretty representative. The spelling and punctuation remains unchanged so that neither the guilty nor the innocent are protected.

## Alisa

*Hi. My name is Alisa. I came from Russia many years ago. I am in very athletic shape, always going to the gym. I like the outdoors, dancing, cooking, bicycling. I have a good sense of humor and am very pretty and considered very attractive and in excellent physical sense.*

*I work as a journalist for a Russian language publication in New York. If you have a moment, pls write.*

*Alisa*


**My observation**:

It's good to know that Alisa is not only very pretty but is also considered to be very attractive. Even more impressive is that she is capable of being both simultaneously at the same time.

Although I'm unclear about what an "excellent physical sense" is, I assume it's probably similar to having common sense but in a well-toned way.

# Anna

*Hi*

*Me call Anna*
*You have interested me.*
*I am sure that you to like much*
*By the girl.*
*And it would be pleasant to me to learn(find out) about you*
*It is more than you have written about yourselves.*
*And you likely too would like to learn(find out)*
*About me more more than here is written.*
*And if you will write to the address*
*Anna197510@Yahoo.com*
*It would be very wonderful and*
*Interestingly not only for me but also*
*For you.*
*Probably that I that girl which*
*You searched.*
*Also there can be you that perfect and*
*Which interesting man I to search.*
*I think, that I am not mistaken with*
*By choice.*
*Also I shall wait with impatience*
*From you yours anyone,*
*The interesting letter.*

*In the large expectation in receptions from you*
*The letters.*
*Necessarily I shall answer any letter.*
*Anna!!!*

## My observation:

It's good to know that Anna will answer any letter. The only question is whether her response will be more decipherable than what she has already offered.

# No Name

*i liked your ad and decided to write you a letter,*

*i am fairly artsy so i do enjoy having dinner parties (i love to cook), painting furniture or rooms, interior decorating, almost anything creative... i love going to dinner, the theater, sporting events, dance clubs, the beach. or staying at home and cooking for someone and then relaxing on the sofa with a movie also is a great way to spend an evening together. I am looking for someone who is open minded and has a healthy sexual attitude.*
*here is my picture click here*

*here is my picture site with me as the main feature lol:*
*click here*
*warning this link is my adults only site!*

*drop me a line if interested... I check mail every few days.*


**My observation:**

Even though the hyperlinks went directly to nude, sexy photos and a subscription-based porn site, she seems to be a lovely lady who likes to do a lot of important things like painting furniture or rooms. Should the occasion arise when I need to have my house painted, she'd be someone to consider because she is one of the few laborers whose work clothes are essentially limited to black lingerie.

## Nikita

*I think you answered my personal ad some time ago,*
*I found your email in my computer...If it is not you I am*
*sorry.*

*If its you I could not answer you because my computer died*
*and I could not get a new one until I get a job or*
*something. I hope you are still interested,*
*as I realize it has been quite awhile.*

*Gosh, I really don't know where to start....*
*maybe you could tell me a little about yourself,*
*how old are you? And what do you look like?*
*And most of all, are you still looking?*

*If you are interested in more about me, I have a*
*Profile at a free site...I did not want to use a pay*
*site because that did not seem like a good*
*thing....Too many of those around.*
*You can check my profile at*

*http://www.alternativepersonals.net*

*I just chose it because you don't have to*
*Pay, and they allow any pictures I want.*
*Oh yea, my username is darla1972.*

*Don't really know what else to say for now*
*Let me know if you are interested, and I hope*
*you don't run when you see my picture:)*

*Bye....Nikits*

**My observation:**

This is one of 3 emails from Nikita – all precisely the same. She really is in a fix with a dead computer and no job. Perhaps, based on our long and committed relationship, she would be willing to accept some money from me so she could repair her computer and we could continue writing. Wait a minute!!! How is she writing emails now???

# Ursula

*Hi, saw your personal profile on the internet, and was wondering if you are interested in meeting someone...I want to make sure I have the right person, and if you are interested before I waste too much time....so I won't get too serious until I hear back from you.*
*Anyhow, my name is Kim, and I am interested in meeting someone for a casual relationship that could lead to more...let me know if you are interested.*

*If I have the wrong person, or you are not interested, then please accept my appolagies, but if so, then let's talk.*

*I have a picture, and profile at:*
*www.adultclassifieds2000.com*
*You can check me out there and see if you are interested as well.*

*Have a great day, Ursula:)*

**My observation:**

It's good that Ursula wants to be certain that I'm the right person – she surely doesn't want to be indiscriminately flashing her private parts for just anyone who happens to be surfing the web. It's comforting to know that discretion is so important to her. It's a good indication that she can be counted on to be a trusted partner in a meaningful relationship.

# Mariya

*Hi, dear,*
*You want to know more about me?........*
*Well, I'm Mariya 45 years old. I'm a writer. I'm writing a fantastic stories. And this is not only my hobby. I've finished the Institute of Radiotechnics and I'm working in the newspaper "Sumskoy Telegraf". I'm a private correspondent there.*

*My society life is full enough but I can't say the same about my private life. I live alone in my own appartments in the centrum of my beautiful city Sumy.*
*And I have a wonderfull dog. His name is Borman.*
*My parents are farmers and they are living in the village 30 km near my city. I have an older brother Alexander. He is 47. He is married with nice woman Zinaida and they are living together with parents. I like to visit them as often as I could . It's so nice to be at the real nature, to feel fresh air, to sweem in the lake and to walk in the forest. Ukrainian nature is too wonderful to be described with the words.*
*But to feel it with all body and spirit it is nessersary to be together with some very close person. Two persons could feel together much much more than one even very romantic....*

*Hope you'll understand me.*
*Mariya*

*P.S. I was never in America or any another country. But I'm interesting in everything new. Please tell me more about your country and your travel exsperiens .*

## My observation:

There seems to be a remarkable similarity between this one and the next email.

## Olga

*Hi, dear,*
*Thank you very much for reply.*
*You want to know more about me.........*

*Well, I'm Olga 45 years old. I'm a writer. I'm writing a fantastic stories. And this is not only my hobby. I've enter Technical University and I'm working in the newspaper " Orion ". I'm a private correspondent there.*

*My society life is full enough but I can't say the same about my private life. I live alone in my own appartments in the centrum of my beautiful city Chernigov. And I have a wonderfull dog. His name is Bublick. My parents are farmers and they are living in the village 80 km near my city.*
*I have an younger brother Alexander. He is 31. He is married with a nice girl Irina and they are living together with parents. I like to visit them as often as I could. It's so nice to be at the real nature, to feel fresh air, to sweem in the lake and to walk inthe forest. Ukrainian nature is too wonderful to be described with the words. But to feel it with all body and spirit it is nessersary to be together with some very close person.*
*Two persons could feel together much much more than one even very romantic....*

*Hope you'll understand me.*
*Olga.*

**My observation:**

Even down to the misspelled words, Olga and Mariya have a lot in common although their wonderful dogs have different names.

The good news is that both have correctly observed that two people together can feel much more romantic than one person together. That's definitely something we would all do well to keep in mind for future relationships.

## Mariya Fedorina

*Hi, dearest,*

*I'm so happy that we found each other that I can't stop writing to you. I'm sorry I've forgot to describe myself.*
*Well, my heigh is 163cm and I'm not very big - 48kg.*
*I have a red hair and my beauty is a real Russian.*
*Any how, I have sent you my picture in previous letter and you could see it yourself. My nationality is Russian but my country is Ukraine. Before it was one very big and very powerfull country USSR. Now there is lot's of small and poor countries. But they are still beautiful and I love my wonderful Ukraine. I hope you'll have one time a possibility to see it with your own eyes.*

*Please tell me about nature and everything you want in your country.*
*Hope to hear from you soon.*
*Mariya*

*My address:*
*Mariya Fedorina*
*Sverdlova str.46, app.22*
*51052 Sumy*
*Ukraine*

*P.S. I don't have too many scanned photos but if you like I could send you some via regular post.*

**My observation:**

Even though I never wrote to her before, I have to admire Mariya's technique of picking up the story as if we are in the middle of corresponding. Unfortunately, it would be impossible for me to become involved with someone who has such poor record-keeping abilities.

# Mariya (again)

*Hi, my dear Prince!*
*Well, you are enough serious.*
*You'd like to have something really serious with me.*
*But first of all we should meet.*
*We must know each other better, we must learn each other.*
*I'm thinking that we feel each other already.*
*Let's deside how could we do that.*
*I'm waiting for your concrete propositions.*
*Mariya*

**My observation:**

I have to give Mariya credit for persistence. Without any encouragement whatsoever, she continues her pursuit. Others may think that this is nothing more than Form Letter #3 but based on our history, I find such a thought to be inconceivable.

I'm concerned that Mariya may not have the necessary funds to afford a trip to the U.S. so that we could feel each other. It might take some convincing but I hope she believes our relationship is enough serious that she'd be willing to at least consider my concrete proposition to send her some money. But she is so damned prideful that getting her to accept my offer will require my most persuasive skills.

# Svetlana

*Hi, dear.*
*Thanks for a letter with your concrete view to our relations. Should we discuss that a bit later? We must decide now something less important but more current.*

*The matter is that I'm not able to pay for the Internet in a moment because yesterday I've lost my second job, which gaves me a possibility to have an Internet. Could you help me in this difficult time? An Internet here in the Ukraine is casts 50 US$ a mounth. Please, send me the money via Western Union Money Transfer. You may get an information about them at www.westernunion.com*

*I've call them today and they told me that to send money you have to go to any of their offices. You have to know an exact name and address (as written in the passport) of the person you are sending money to.*
*Svetlana Aroyko*
*Gogolya str.12, app.33*
*Chernigov*
*Ukraine*

*I'm so sorry that I'm asking you about that but I have nobody else to ask about this...... By chance it would be that guarantee I was asked you about. I meen that if you are really need me you'll help me with my problems.*
*And this is very normal.*

*If you are really serious to me, please send me in your next e-mail a transmission number from the Western Union.*
*And we will have still a fast way (Internet) to talk.*
*Hope to hear from you.*
*Svetlana*
       *P.S. And I really hope that one day I'll have a chance to do something for us as well.*

**My observation:**

Poor Svetlana. She really is stuck and has no one else to turn to. As soon as I get around to it, I'll send her the money so we can continue the conversation that we never began.

# Howie says "No"

More often than not, to the surprise of absolutely no one, there comes a time – usually quite early - when there is little need to continue an email conversation.

The easy way out is to simply not respond. An unanswered inquiry is clearly understood. It may not be preferred but it is definitive. And doing nothing requires absolutely no effort whatsoever.

Because many participants in online searches are sending out a number of trial balloons, most of their attention is spent on the people who continue to participate. The ones that drop out or who never reply are unlikely to be missed.

Nevertheless, for me the guilt/rudeness factor was always in play. So, as often as possible, I chose to avoid the "I pass" option of doing nothing and, instead, chose the slightly more uncomfortable path of explaining why I was opting out.

The relatively obvious excuse ("you're ugly, stupid or boring", while often apt, didn't feel like an acceptable option.

Although I often had a good reason to end something that had barely begun (especially when my relationship with Debbie was beginning to build so positively) I still felt uncomfortable about sending off a "form" response. True, the gist of my replies was essentially the same but I felt the need to at least indicate that I had actually read the emails that had been sent to me.

In other words, I felt the need to say no. But, even though I knew it was more than likely that the recipient would take a "who cares?" attitude, I still wanted to bow out with at least some semblance of dignity.

Sometimes it took a few exchanges before I knew it was time to say goodbye. Often, however, I didn't even have time to say hello. What follows is a sampling of the early endings, beginning as usual, with a response to my Profile.

# Barbara

*Hi H,*

*I think you have the funniest profile that I've ever read. Well, maybe one of the top two or three. I like to think that I'm both funny and smart. People have told me this, but of course, people lie, so you'll have to be the judge. And it's hard to be funny in an email, especially an email to a total stranger. (Are you totally strange?)*

*Well, if we go to France, I can probably help out a little with the language, (a very little) but if we go to the South, I don't think I'll be much help there. One of the funniest conversations that I ever eavesdropped on (I love listening in to what other people are saying; I know it's not nice, but I do) was a conversation between a man and a woman in a diner in some small town in Tennessee. She had a French accent and he spoke Southern English. I don't think either one of them understood anything that the other was saying. So hopefully, there was something else going in that relationship, because neither was looking for smart, funny and witty, believe me.*

*Well, what else would you like to know about me, besides the fact that I have a tendency to ramble and make a lot of typos when I'm typing this time of night? (Oh, that's right, you can't see the typos because I'm correcting them.)*

*What do you do with the cockroaches? The other day I was riding my exercise bicycle (you gotta do something to keep the "middle age spread" in check) and watching the new version of "To Tell The Truth." I'd never seen it and I never watch TV during the day, but riding that bicycle can be deadly, let me tell you. You don't even get to feel the wind through your hair. Anyway, the people being interviewed were trying to impress upon the panel that they made little dolls out of cockroaches. (Of course, only one of them actually did that; the other two were pretenders, but you knew that.) And they actually had samples. Cute samples. Not that I'd want one in my house but the roaches were dead. And baked. And dressed up. Oh,you get the picture. So what do you do with yours?*

*Well, that's it for now. Oh, I guess I should tell you some of the basics about me. I'm 51 years old, I'm a high school social studies teacher (been doing it for what seems like forever, at this point, but it's only be 24 years) and I have two grown children, who are on their own (thank goodness, I've finished paying for college). I'm a widow, have been for almost six years, and I've decided at long last that I'm kind of ready to see the world again. So here I am.*

*Listen, do me a favor. Even if you're not interested, or otherwise engaged, at least drop me a line and say so. I hate it when people ignore my email.*

*Oh, I'll attach a picture of myself so you can get an idea of what I look like. (I also look like Paul Newman.)*

*Barbara*


Hi Barbara -

Thanks for you note. I was happy to hear that I made the top 3 of the funniest profiles you've ever read. But there was a note of disappointment as well - dropping from #1 to merely being a bronze medal winner was quite a blow.

I'm right with you about eavesdropping. One of my favorite pastimes is picking up on the snippets of conversation when I pass people who are walking in the opposite direction. Usually I end up hearing no more than a sentence - and then I try to figure out what they could possibly have been discussing to cause that sentence to occur. Here's one: "The last time my brother came here to visit, a dead pigeon fell out of the sky...and landed on his head." That's something I'm not used to hearing on everyday basis.

I think I'm going to have to take up another activity relating to cockroaches: collecting stories. So far, thanks to you, cockroach dolls in designer clothes will be the first entry.

Howie

**Note:**

Somehow through sloth, incompetence or total lack of technical acumen – and quite possibly all three - I have managed to misplace Barbara's next email. The only thing I'm able to determine is that she must have mentioned something about my willingness to do dishes which prompted this response from me.

Miss B –

I neglected to mention that, in addition to being able to wash AND dry, I am also quite capable of picking up a phone and ordering from a complex menu. On occasion, I have even been known to fetch the meal or reward the deliverer with gratitude and a meaningful tip. Sometimes, admittedly rare, I have been known to transfer the restaurant fare onto presentable platters. Usually though, I'll just eat from the plastic plate in which the meal arrives – often with a single utensil. Just because I'm a whiz at doing dishes is no reason I need to practice my craft on a daily basis.

As much as I enjoy our back and forth, the timing is less than ideal. After an uncountable number of false starts and uncomfortable misses, I have now begun to see someone and, although we are not yet written in the Big Book, there is reason to believe that we are in the early stages of what may - if nobody (probably me) screws it up - potentially be a real, honest-to-goodness, adult relationship. I've been known to drop this ball badly in the past but I'm doing my best to stay focused this time.

I wish you well.

Howie


*hi howie,*

*just wanted to say thank you for answering my letter, even though you've found someone that you enjoy spending time with. i hope it works out. i can understand not wanting to see more than one person at a time. i don't think i could do that either.*

*actually, your ad was the funniest one i've read, but i didn't want to be too flattering, at least not at first.*

*good luck, and if you ever want to write again, feel free to do so.*
*barbara*

# Belinda

*H –*

*I enjoyed your profile immensely!! I even shared it with my co-worker. We howled. Maybe we can meet for a cup of coffee sometime and chat.*
*Belinda*
Hi Belinda –

Glad to hear that I was able to bring some levity to you and your co-worker. While I'm not sure that howling in the office is the road to professional success, it's always nice to be appreciated – or laughed at.

My situation is somewhat changed. I have met several women on Match.com with varying degrees of predictable failure. While some were near-disasters, others were simply connections that never should have been made. But, as I pressed on, amazingly (at least to me) I did meet someone. Although we're hardly in the throes of an exclusive, committed relationship, at least for now it seems that we're where we're supposed to be. So, meeting someone new – for coffee, a chat or anything else – just doesn't feel right.

Thanks for your note. I wish you well.

Howie

# E

*Greetings:*

*Nobody on Match ever says they're an atheist!!! Well, I do, but it is very rare. Ten days in Philly? Winters in Santa Barbara?*

*Tell me more.*

*I've been in Philly 18 years, teaching at Drexel (history). This is a great city.*

*E.*


Hi E –

One of the reasons – in fact the main reason – I was so clear about my irreligious attitudes in my profile is that, although getting back into the dating cycle has its benefits, I believe that getting the important deal breakers in play as soon as possible avoids wasting anyone's time.

I see, by your Profile, that you are equally clear. That's the good news and the bad news.

In many ways, we are certainly compatible. But in others, the chasm is wide. You are an outside person. I'm really not. While your idea of a great day is cycling, hiking or being on the open water, my idea of a great day is enjoying the outdoors by looking through a window. I'm an inside person. In the fall, I go to Elk Lake with my friends. They spend the entire day wandering the mountain trails and wondering why I remain in the cabin endlessly putting more wood on the fire. They walk. I write. They fish. I read. They go to bed early. I come alive when night falls.

In other words, I fear that I'd be an anchor to you or you'd carry more guilt than necessary for dragging me into a world that I've been trying to avoid.

Howie

# Naomi

*Hi:*

*You really could pass for 65 and a half! I love your sense of humor.*

*Are you looking for an atheist? I have some of the same reservations about religion that you do, particularly where it goes to extremes, but I'm tolerant of the myths people hold to if it improves their lives without hurting others.*

*Read my profile and tell me what you think. If you think the religion thing is an unbridgeable gap, let me know.*

*My best,*

*Naomi*


Hi Naomi –


Thanks for your note.

I'm not so impassioned about non-religion as I am about people who feel the need to impose their religion on others. I also find it peculiar that believers are so thankful to God for the good things that occur but turn a blind eye to the evil that surrounds them. I'm currently on a business trip in Chicago where a huge fire has completely torched one of the city's oldest and most beloved churches. Somehow very few people are thanking God for the tragedy. Maybe He did it by accident.

On to more important things. My guess is that your experience with Match.com somewhat mirrors mine. For the most part it's been pretty disappointing. But not always. I was surprised – and pleased – to meet someone I actually want to see again. And, although our status is relatively new, we are in the early stages of something that holds at least a modicum of potential. Given that glimmer of hope, I'm no longer continuing to meet other people.

In other words, the timing for you and me is less than ideal. I wish you well.

Howie

# Milan

*Dear Paul, Dear Brad, Oh must be mistaken!!*

*If you need a guide, I'm your Philly girl. I know the Philly Y, (check the map!). It's your call if you find me smart or Phunny, but my Philly Phunnies have zinged me.*

*Know where to eat, what to avoid and have even dabbled in R.E. I can say you'awl but need some help with espanol, francais, Deutsch and Italiano.*

*Not sure who is older, U or me, but I'm a spring chicken. I'm rarely shy, Philly sarcastic, and read a lot to help the brain -not sure if it's worked yet. So the pun is on you, if you intend it or not.*

*From a city in Italy*


Hi Milan –

For the record, the word is "y'all" not "you'awl". And, for further edification, y'all is singular. When speaking to a group, the phrase is "all y'all". It's no wonder those in the speech-impaired South voted against Obama. I hope he cuts off their food stamps.

Thanks for your note. As they say in areas other than Dixie, you got style.

They also say timing is everything. Ours is less than ideal. After putting in the requisite time meeting lots of Ms. Wrong, somehow I seem to have met a Ms. Maybe. While we're hardly at the moment when the relationship is being documented in indelible ink, we are moving in a positive direction. And, even though I'm not yet a fully credentialed grown up, I am adult enough to know that there is a time when straying off the straight and narrow is likely to cause problems. So, though tempted, I'm toeing the line.

I wish you happiness. Or whatever else you prefer.

Howie

# The Great Motivator. Sex.

For me, the reason to enter the world of internet dating wasn't very complicated. There was, of course, the ultimate goal of finding a life partner – someone with whom to share joys, tears, highs, lows and the inevitable surplus of lackluster, forgettable moments. Someone who would, when push came to shove, change my adult diapers, and never call attention to my one or two very minor foibles that are annoying to the point of crazy-making.

Those were indeed all worthy goals and certainly high on my list of considerations. But there was a far greater reason to begin the search. Although companionship would be nice, a little sexual satisfaction in the meantime couldn't hurt.

So, even though sex was unmentioned on my Internet Profile, in both the back and front of my mind, getting laid was a high priority. OK … the highest priority.

Online dating seems to have been invented for people like me. People for whom fear of rejection makes it so much easier to not even make an effort. Spurred by the preconceived assurance that since she'd probably say "no" anyway, I don't even bother to ask the question. So predictably, I almost always left a party or some social event without a woman but with any number of male friends who, like me, were able to come up with multiple excuses for our ineptitude.

But the internet changed everything. That's because in cyberspace rejection is essentially anonymous and therefore painless.

Getting turned down in person can be embarrassing, depressing and emotionally crippling. But the anonymity of the internet removes the sting from even the most gentle rebuff.

Online personas are fully armored; fully protected. Until names, addresses and contact information is exchanged, when you're online you don't have to be who you really are. You can be whoever you say you are.

The phrase "She doesn't know me from Adam" is absolutely correct. Actually, there's almost a 100% chance that she doesn't even know Adam.

So, for me, the internet offered promise of a safe haven – well at least a much safer haven. The goal posts hadn't been moved but the stigma for a lack of scoring came with significantly diminished humiliation.

Thus armed, I began my sexual foray into the online wilderness.

# A philosophical overview of sex and a few uncomfortable personal stories.

For those whose sexual awakening took place many years ago when Free Love meant something other than "no cash required", sex was always an important part of life. Of course, that importance diminished over time as children were born and the thrill of waking up next to the same wrinkled person lost its titillating edge. Nevertheless, when circumstances changed and mature adults like me found ourselves once again venturing onto the dating scene, no topic was more top of mind.

Sexually speaking, everyone is concerned about everything. Is mine a body that anyone will find appealing when naked? Do I remember what to do? How to start? What to say? And the most pressing question: when is too soon, when is not soon enough and how is the subject even broached in the first place?

If the mere idea of dating for the first time in years is concerning – and it almost assuredly is – then the thought of having sex takes discomfort to an even more intimidating level. The good news is that once you get started, just like riding a bike, it all comes back surprisingly easily. Especially if you were an excellent bike rider.

## The Sexual Divide

Everybody believes they have a good sense of humor. But you know from personal experience that's a huge exaggeration.

Sex is a lot like that. There are very few who regard themselves as inadequate sexual partners. Which means that a lot of people are terribly wrong.

Adding to the difficulty is that, for the most part, sex involves two people. There are numerous exceptions, and you should feel free to fill in your own diversions, but for purposes of this discussion let's remain in the mainstream and limit the topic to a pair of naked individuals.

Let's start with the basics: sexual compatibility is critical. In other words, it helps to be on the same wavelength. You like this? Good, I can do that. You don't like this? OK, I won't do it anymore.

But sometimes it's simply hopeless. Energies, subtleties, appetites, peculiarities and much, much more are monumentally diverse. Sad but true, some couples are never going to enjoy good sex. Each of the participants may have experienced ecstatic fulfillment with someone else, but, as a couple, they need to face the fact that, together, they will be unable to make orgasmic lemonade.

Both sadly and happily, I speak from experience. I've been the good partner and the poor craftsman who left the job unacceptably completed. And I carry the gnawing suspicion that the women who have found me to be less than ideal have - both before and after me - enjoyed wonderful sex with someone else.

The old saw invariably holds true: it's not you; it's me.

So when the sexual bridge was crossed, either the gold stars came out or a felt tipped pen drew a big black "X" through a name and phone number that was sometimes hers and, just as often mine.

**You're doing it wrong**

You know the old saying "what's good for the goose is good for the gander"? Don't count on it.

Ganders are easily satisfied. Did I get off? OK, I'm good. But every goose has her own requirements. And even though the rules are seldom spelled out in advance, non-compliance is seldom an acceptable option.

Basic rule: nobody's perfect and everybody's different. Roughly translated that means just because you've had satisfactory relationships in the past there is no reason to think that the happy ride will continue with your next partner. And all it takes is one turn-off to ruin the party.
Some women think it's sexy when you take their clothes off. Others would much rather take responsibility for wardrobe removal. The way you'll learn the preferred method is almost certainly by doing the wrong one.

As the action progresses, opportunities for pleasure and displeasure abound. Just because you don't hear "don't do that" doesn't mean you're on the right track. Chances are you're not.

There's an old saying that good sex is good but bad sex is …well, even bad sex can be pretty good, too. Nope. Bad sex is just plain wrong even though it's likely to occur more often than most of us are willing to admit.

**Do you have a ladder or something?**

If there is something that in your wildest dreams you cold never conceive, rest assured that there is a website devoted to it. And there are thousands of appreciative followers who visit those sites on a daily basis.

If you've heard of something you feel is peculiar, deranged or perhaps even physically inconceivable, you can be confident that it's probably taking place right now. And quite possibly right next door.

There is a reason why every year at the NAB (National Association of Broadcasters) Convention in Las Vegas, there are two enormous floors devoted to the newest film, TV and video releases. Because this is the biggest event of its kind, the venue is massive. On the first floor in extravagantly designed, spacious and lavishing furnished booths are executives, representatives and celebrities from every major film studio and television network as well as a seemingly unlimited number of representatives from a variety of independent entertainment companies. The display is so overwhelming that even a full day's commitment may be insufficient to experience all there is to see.

The entire second floor – precisely the same size – is dedicated to porn. Nothing but porn.

It's OK if you're not OK with that but take this as fair warning: don't be surprised to learn that your new partner believes that the missionary position is best left to missionaries.

What is acceptable and what is not requires a majority vote – something often difficult to achieve when there are only two people at the ballot box. If the division is 50-50, by decree you don't have to compromise. But if you don't, there are almost certain to be repercussions. The phrase "don't let the doorknob hit you in the ass when you leave" is highly likely to be in your immediate future.

My experience – or more accurately, my inexperience - was all too apparent on all too many occasions. One woman was not just surprised - she was actually stunned - to learn that I had no KY Jelly in the medicine cabinet or, even more importantly, conveniently stored in a bedside cabinet where it would be handy and ready for use should she be overcome by a desire to flip over. That relationship

180

eventually failed for a number of reasons although none of them were necessarily tied to her desired port of entry.

As to the aforementioned ladder, the answer is yes, it was definitely requested. Until then, I had foolishly thought its value in my bedroom was limited to gaining access to books placed on a high shelf. Silly, practical, me. It turns out that with some imagination, a bit of dexterity and no fear of heights, ladders have other, more carnal, functionalities.

Ladders, needless to say, are just a warm up. Apparently the traditional American home is awash with optional sexual equipment that has hitherto been limited to much more mundane uses.

Unarmed, unaware and undaunted, I felt totally prepared to see what awaited me in the sexual wilderness I was about to enter. Not surprisingly, what occurred turned out to be both more and less than I anticipated.

# A Memorable Maiden Voyage

It began the way all the others began – with a response to my online Profile:

*may i say that your personal was a most refreshing change from the majority that i have read.........i would love to chat with you, perhaps online?......i am both witty and intelligent and i must admit, it is a change to find a man who is the proud possessor of both attributes......i am putting you on my buddy list and will look for you ........if that is not possible, please advise and i will provide you with a most informative bio!!......ciao*

Didi was the first. The first to respond. The first I engaged in an on-going email correspondence. The first to arouse my interest.

And, as it turned out, she aroused a lot more than that.

For a first experience, it was great. Good opening. Good story. Big crescendo leading to a memorable ending.

Didi actually saw my Profile before it was even officially posted. But if, like me, you're from the 60's and you're inclined to go with the flow, you'll understand why I took that as a good sign.

I'm still not sure how that happened. When I wrote the profile for AOL Personals, I was informed that it would take about 5 days before it would go online.

There are surely reasons for a 5-day delay, but I don't really understand what they might be – other than the need to check for improprieties. Even so, it's hard to think of what might be considered improper. There seem to be some pretty promiscuous profiles already on view. But, I guess in the world of true porn, the AOL site really is pretty tame.

Nevertheless, long before the 5 days were up, Didi responded.

I checked AOL to find my Profile, but it simply wasn't there. I had attempted to attach a photo – and learned that it would take and additional 2 weeks to accomplish such a monumental task. I was also informed that my method of sending a photo was incompatible with AOL's system. That was tragic news. I knew the depth of that tragedy because AOL had been kind enough to let me know that my ad would have a 5 times better chance of being viewed if it contained a photograph.

Frankly, based on personal experience, I think their estimate was a bit low. Everyone looks at the photo first. Rule of thumb:  No photo, no interest.

My technological ineptitude is legendary.  I was completely stymied. But if there is one lesson I have learned about computers it's this: when in doubt, re-boot. And, because I didn't know what else to do, I re-sent the same photo the same way. This time, AOL was delighted to post it. I didn't care that they offered no explanation because I was already feeling successful.

Back to Didi.

She followed her first response with a second one that included her profile.

A portion:

*... as promised, here is a short synopsis of "me"--------i am 50, italian-jewish, reside on the north shore of LI........i am ivy educated(vassar/cornell law), 5'5, thick shiny dark hair, big brown eyes, high cheekbones and olive skin......i am not*

*a skinny mannequin, but a voluptuous and fit woman......i am told that my face is a combination of sophia lorens and julia louis dreyfuss......i am quite witty, classy, charismatic and of course romantic............*

Certainly promising.

And, since at that point, there was no one else in the game, it was easy to begin corresponding with her. My response:

Miss D –

Well...that isn't a bio; it's an enticement. What about the not so good parts - the "once in a while I eat my young" or the "I am the mother of the PMS Syndrome"?

Unlike most people, I have nothing bad to say about lawyers. Because I earned my living doing advertising and writing for film and TV, there's not much room for me to criticize any profession. One of the books that I am writing is being done in collaboration with a lawyer from Chicago and he is one of the smartest and most ethical people I know.

I also can't match your physical appearance. In contrast to your thick, shiny hair, I have none. Well, at least none on the top of my head. I'm not skinny either, but I've been eating a lot healthier and working out a bit lately, so at least I'm not wearing my chubby clothes.

Have I moved the ball sufficiently?

Howie

Later on, and still relatively early in the process, I did get some other responses. All of them – other than Didi's – seemed to fall into one of two categories:

## 1.  The sneak attack

These emails usually began with an abundant usage of the word "discrete". In my mind, I pictured a very timid woman, venturing into the vast, mysterious internet wonderland with more than a bit of trepidation. In my mind I could almost see one woman blush as she explained that she was married to a man who simply was uninterested in sex. So, with great apprehension, she decided to test other waters. She was looking for a discrete relationship with someone who could respect that she was a married woman.

Because she was familiar with the importance of including more than verbal information, she also offered a hyperlink to a website that promised to display her photo.

A check of that site revealed several photographs of the demure angel. It wasn't quite what I had envisioned although it was probably what I should have expected. She was nude, directly facing the camera with both feet locked above her head, while she spread herself with both hands.

So much for discretion.

## 2. The Russian Connection

Apparently there is an abundance of Russian women who are desperate to meet American men. Some want passage to America. Some want husbands. Most are willing to settle for cash.

They write with varying degrees of competence in the English language. But what they lack in grammatical skills is more than compensated for with directness. Their sentence structure may be iffy but their message is abundantly clear. Often they include photos – usually in suggestive poses.

For reasons that I cannot completely justify, I decided to answer the first one I received. I was new to the cyber-dating game so I think initially I responded to anyone who showed interest. I'm certain, however, that my response was, although kind, certainly pretty clear – I wasn't in the market for anyone who didn't live in New York City.

I didn't hear anything for a while, but eventually a response appeared.

The note began, "My dearest darling…". It then went on to explain that life for her had become difficult. Unfortunately, she had lost her job and was unable to afford her internet service, thereby making it impossible to continue our wonderful relationship. She suggested that I might want to pay for the service and could do so by wiring the money directly to the provider.

Almost immediately, there was a second email. She had just learned, much to her great distress, that the internet provider could not accept money from me. It would have to come directly from her. So, although she would have preferred some other way, the only option was for me to wire the money to her home.

Even for someone as obtuse as I can often be, the scam seemed pretty obvious. I appreciated the inventiveness and creativity but not sufficiently to send money.

Compared to the scammers who had targeted me as a potential sucker, Didi had a leg up. As it turned out, she was interested in having both of her legs up. That specific information came somewhat later but in the meantime her correspondence was encouraging…

*... you have indeed moved that ball with a most interesting diatribe!!!.... i no longer practice the legal arts but instead i am a writer......my agent is in soho, another wonderful part of the city...... the north shore of LI can only be likened to a town called "stepford" from the movie "the stepford wives"....... needless to say, i fit in here like a pork chop on passover!!!...... i would say that my biggest fault at this early hour is petulance!!!......no pms(a blessing from above)......... by the way, what do you like?.....what really gets your blood boiling?......thats it, no more deposing from me...........your turn!........D...........p.s. do you have a name?*

Our email exchanges began somewhat tentatively and continued on that level until they took a sharp right turn when she offered some startling information in the middle of an otherwise chatty note.

*howie........you truly are a most interesting man......... you are correct in your assessment of arrogance and stupidity.......in my genre(lawyers) that combination is quite prevalent!!!.............i still live here because of my daughter and other reasons, which will be mentioned at another time......i have written a first time novel which is in the process of hopefully being converted to another venue(which you and i could really discuss based on your interests)....separated for one year and CELIBATE BY CHOICE for 7 years.......i know i know, you must be reeling with that comment.........long story, perhaps for an in person discussion.....i am enjoying our bantering via email, but perhaps, if i am bold in this request, it would be lovely to speak via telephone sometime..... my name is Didi.........ciao*

It wasn't the kind of information I was expecting. 7 years is a very long time. Most of the people I know who have been celibate for 7 years are about 7 years old.

So, obviously, this was a subject that needed to be explored.

It turns out that Didi has been separated for a year. Given that the relationship had been in demise, several months of celibacy could be accounted for. But what about the other months – and all of the remaining 6 years of her marriage?

Didi brushed off that question with ease. At some point in their marriage, her husband realized that he was gay. She didn't specify the precise moment that became apparent but, using my auspicious subtraction skills, I concluded that it was not a recent occurrence.

Other details:

He still hasn't told their 15 year-old daughter about his homosexuality. Even though he lives with his lover in Brooklyn Heights. Even though he is very close to his daughter and has taken her to Europe with him. Even though he is very involved in her life.

But enough about him.

The next obvious question is: Why stay in a marriage with a gay man? The answer: come on, let's all say it together: "for the children." Or, in this case, for the child.

One daughter. Fifteen years old. Adopted.

Admittedly, there is some fuzziness in the time line here, but let's go on, shall we? Just take it as gospel that for Didi there were no inters coursing during the final years of her marriage.

But, and this is somewhat out of sequence, although it does lead naturally into the true story of Didi, it turns out that while Mr. Fudgepacker had no interest in traditional intercourse or, more specifically, in the missionary position, he was, in fact very willing participant in oral sex. To be even more specific, he was willing to put his mouth where her money is.

Apparently there are Gay men and there are gay Men.

It might be reasonable to question how I was able to possess such personal information after only an early exchange of emails? The answer: I wouldn't.

But, as soon as we switched from the computer to the telephone (a progression that took place relatively quickly) the subject matter intensified as did the pace with which it was provided.

The first call came from Didi.

For those unfamiliar with online dating, I offer this brief lesson in internet protocol:

Once the subject of an actual phone conversation has been breached, the question immediately arises: who offers a phone number? Remember, this was the early days of the internet. Remember also the scary stories about cyber stalkers. Although we may all know some people who have not only met online but have also formed lasting relationships, we also know there is danger out there. And, until this point, everything has taken place relatively anonymously and only via computers. So if there is an expressed desire to move on to the next plateau, it's usually up to the guy to offer his phone number. It's not only the gentlemanly thing to do – it also seems the safest way for the woman to take the next step.

Didi suggested the phone. I gave her my number. She called from her cell while she was at a Farmers Market. That gave her an opportunity to provide me with complete descriptions about the tomatoes and the age, size and disposition of the women who were sharing the shopping experience with her. The long and short of it is that all of them are old and short.

Nevertheless, the banter was good. It was light and about nothing of consequence. The conversation was easy, comfortable and fun.

But the discussion changed when she got to the grapefruit section. From there she offered an observation about the ruby red giant grapefruit, "These are big, but my breasts are bigger."

This information was immediately followed by some even more suggestive visions until she realized that the diminutive, elderly women who overheard the conversation were not as appreciative an audience as I had just become. Perhaps one of them even expressed displeasure. Perhaps the censure came from the woman who works the cash register.

Although I was unsure of the specifics, it was clear that *someone* certainly offered a stinging comment. And Didi was quick to offer her candid evaluation of the individual, "That cunt."

Of course she immediately followed with an explanation that she is not a big fan of the "C" word. If that were the case, she'd be the first woman I've ever met who is.

But, she explained, on occasion, it is the correct word. Who am I to disagree? I like women who talk dirty.

It was at this precise moment that the quality of our exchanges took a definitive turn in the direction of sexuality. And it turned out to be a subject from which we never veered. Never.

Although the emails continued, from that first phone call onward, they played a much more limited role. There is a "good morning" email from Didi every day and a return note from me, but the telephone has now become our weapon of choice.

Didi –

.... By all means, if you have time tonight, call. I'll be home, finishing the writing that I didn't get done because some woman called me from the fruit stand and kept me on the phone talking about her big ruby grapefruits.

Howie


The phone calls occur nightly. They last at least an hour and sometimes much longer. The subject matter, for almost the entire duration is, in a word, sex.

I'd never had phone sex before. I wasn't against it. It just never occurred to me. Usually, if I am having sex, I'm glad to be having sex – and I'm glad it's with the person who's sharing my bed. That's <u>why</u> we're having sex. We like each other and we like being together. And, because we are physically together the phone doesn't seem particularly necessary. Additionally, we're together often enough to satisfy my sex drive. I'm not 18 anymore, so my need to have sex is limited to considerably less than 3 times a day. When I'm out of town, I'm usually not away very long. And, quite often when I'm away, the person I'm having sex with is away with me. And because she is, we continue to have sex.

And, just between us girls, the idea of calling someone I don't know to have a sexy conversation just never seemed like a reasonable way to pass the time. That's why according to Scripture, on the 8th day, the Lord invented porno flicks.

So, when it comes to phone sex, I'm a complete virgin.

Still, I _am_ willing to learn. It is a burden, but for the right cause, I'm willing to make the sacrifice.

And, to be honest, this feels pretty damned cool. Because, in addition to the very graphic sexual conversations, there's all this mystery about who Didi is and what she looks like.
So, we talk. First it's about her years of celibacy. A reasonable first question: did she miss the sex? After all, sexuality and sensuality can diminish without constant stimulation. I know lots of women who, by choice, have been celibate for a year or even longer. In some ways they miss being sexually active, but in many others, they're fine with where they are. They know it's not going to last forever. And, after the (choose 1 or more) man who couldn't commit, the man who wouldn't commit, the man whose mother ruled his life, the man whose children ruled his life, the gambler, the drunk, the philanderer or the whatever, there is certain pleasure to be derived from taking matters of sexual release into your own hands.

But that's not the case. Didi continues to feel like a very sexual woman - a woman who is very much aware of what is being missed. It's incredibly important to her. She's frustrated, angry, upset, confused and desperate about her sexual inactivity. It's all she thinks about. She's bored with masturbation. She's had it up to here with vibrators. She's ready for the real thing. In fact, she's more than ready. Ready was last year. There are no words to describe the badly chewed shape of the bit at which she is presently chomping.

Sex is pretty much all she talks about. To me, that's not such a bad thing. While it will probably come as no great surprise to anyone, guys appreciate a woman who talks about what turns her on.

So, we keep talking. As the subject matter gets more and more explicit, I find myself asking lots of questions. The main question is, "I wonder what will happen if I were to move the conversation to an even more erotic direction. I wonder if she'll go, for example, … here?"

The answer is, "yes".

I can't pick a topic that she doesn't want to discuss. In depth. And in excruciating detail.

Here's a for instance: Ménage a trois.

That's never been a fantasy of mine. My attitude is that it's pretty much all I can do to satisfy one woman. Why would I want two? What would I do? Even a cursory check of available equipment shows that I have an insufficient tool supply.

But Didi is convincing. And, as she explains her attitude and responsibilities, I begin to see her point. Maybe I could do this. Especially, if it's her fantasy. After all, I'd be doing her a favor. So if it's something she really, really wants, I should at least be willing to help. That's just the kind of guy I am.

She continues her description and I continue to warm to the possibility. Didi notes that the other woman would have to be someone special. But it's important that she is someone safe, someone Didi knows. There is a pause while she thinks. Then, "I know who I'd like to bring."

Well now we've moved the fantasy pretty far. Because now we're talking specifics. Of course I don't know the other woman – to be perfectly accurate, I don't even know Didi – but this discussion has a ring of reality. A fantasy is "in your dreams." This now looms as an actual possibility or, better yet, an eventuality.

By this point we've had many conversations and we're well into the specifics of when we're going to get together. The details have to do with timing – the location has been clear from the beginning. Because Didi has a daughter who lives at home, we'll meet at my house.

That's fine with me. More than fine.

For the first time, Didi expresses some hesitation. It results in a minor flurry of emails.

*Howie –*

*... I'm concerned that you're expecting a runway model which I'm definitely not. What if you don't like the way I look...?*

*Didi*

Didi –

... would it be too much to ask you to lose, say, 30 or 40 pounds, before we meet next week?  What if I send you some photos of the body styles I prefer and you can sculpt yourself to conform to them? Perhaps you could visit the local drive-thru Liposuction Hut and be thin by supper.  You might want to check out the new book "How Bulimia Helped Me Get My Man." There are plenty of acceptable diuretics on the market.  Starvation diets work well - believe me, Ghandi was not considered a sexpot "Before." And if all else fails, you can always fall back on vertical stripes. Or you can blindfold me before you tie me up. There are so many possibilities.

Relax.

Howie

*howie*

*...you are SO cute!!!...*

*D*


Didi -

I left out Mumu's, distorted camera lenses, posing with cheeks sucked in, and the most obvious solution: simply transferring your head to another body.

There are so many opportunities...why not try them all?

Howie

*h*

*... this time you really have out-done yourself...*

*Didi –*


Miss D –

The issue is not whether I have outdone myself. Doing or outdoing me has never been the issue. The real question is, after 7 years, who is going to do you?

Howie


Back to timing. When will we actually get together?

We talk about several possibilities, but settle on Friday (about 3 days away). Although it's unspoken, there is no question that she'll spend the night. I even suggest that, because she is going to be in the city on Thursday to have dinner with girlfriends, she might consider coming to my apartment afterwards. That way we could get together a day earlier. She's up for that. By the time the phone call ends, we're leaning towards Thursday.

Those plans fall apart by morning.

Didi has a cousin who is an entertainment lawyer and he has shown some of his friends a few of the early scenes from a screenplay she has written. The friends are very important Hollywood agents who have big-time connections.

These agents want to meet with her and they have a brief opening in their schedule. Her cousin thinks she should immediately take advantage of their interest. Who knows when they'll be able to see her if she misses this opportunity? If she can get to LA by the weekend, they'll meet.

Life immediately changes. Didi has packing to do – and before that, shopping. She'll be flying to L.A. on Wednesday morning and won't return until early Sunday morning.

It's not a problem – just a delay. So we move our proposed meeting date back a few days and I make alternate Friday night plans. Depending on how exhausted she is, she'll try to come over in the afternoon on Sunday. Monday, at the very latest. It's hardly crisis time.

Didi sends me an email. The background color is bright, electric pink.

*howie........just thought i would try this color........i just finished working out and am now heading to the nail salon to get waxed, plucked, fondled and painted!!!.....i will try to call you before i leave........remember, i will have my pc with me so i can send email and my cell phone.......you have entrance to both mediums.....(soon, you shall have*

*entrance to my medium!!!, or is that large????)i must tell*
*you that you do make me smile......D*


Miss D -

Yikes. That color certainly is a wake-up call. But pink is certainly an appropriate color, given our discussions.

Entrance to your medium...large? I thought you told me that you were tight. This is much too confusing for me. I guess I'll just have to wait and check it out myself. And I promise you, I'll be checking very, very closely.

H


Here's a shocker. The Hollywood plans fall through. Her trip is cancelled, and Didi is outraged. While I never fully understand the reasons for the cancellation, I'm even more mystified by her reaction.

For reasons that have not been entirely grounded in reality, Didi has been counting on this meeting as her Big Break. That a meeting scheduled so quickly would need to be changed had never occurred to her. That this meeting was only going to be a preliminary discussion never occurred to her. All she knows is that her world has fallen completely apart. She is angry, hurt, frustrated, bitter, frantic and extremely vocal.

As we talk on the phone, I try to explain what should have been painfully obvious: getting a Hollywood deal is a long, involved, complex process. Didi is an attorney – she's not unsophisticated and she's certainly not dumb. So it struck me as surprising that she would have placed so much importance on such a relatively innocuous meeting. Long planned Hollywood deals involving powerful people fall through with regularity. But this wasn't even a deal. This was a very preliminary early get-together. Even worse, it was a get together with agents. Certainly, having an agent is important – but simply having a representative is a long way from having a deal. It's a step, and an important one. But if writing a book is step 1 and having a film made is step 100, getting an agent is no more than step 3. I'm bored with this lesson in Hollywood deal-making too. Back to the sex.

Didi doesn't think that I ought to break my Friday night plans. I'd rather not break them either. But, for obvious reasons, I'm more than willing. You know the old saying about a bush in the hand...There is still Thursday. After the dinner with her girlfriends, she could certainly come over. But Didi is no longer into that scenario. So, we come up with new plan:she'll come to my place on Saturday afternoon.

In one of her emails, Didi explains that she is all "a twitter" about the impending events. When I tell her that I share the enthusiasm, she jokingly questions whether I am taking things for granted. By now, the ball is not only rolling downhill in a most specific direction, the speed has accelerated to avalanche proportions. There is nothing to be taken for granted here – what is about to occur is inevitable. Nevertheless, I respond:

Didi -

Of course I was not referring to sexual tension as it might relate to us. It was meant more as an amplification of the word "a-twitter". I am with you regarding the impending direction of our relationship. It will be completely platonic; the sleepovers accomplished in separate beds whilst garbed in layers upon layers of pajamas, bathrobes and who knows what else. What could ever have led you to believe that there could conceivably be any other direction...other than the hours of talk about years of sexual deprivation, the long involved descriptions about oral sex - both with and without piercings, the deep and involved explanations about genital sizes (including your own), boredom with masturbation, shared visits to porn sites on the web, and shared, simultaneous viewings of Real Sex on HBO.

But the idea of you and I having sex? Please. It never crossed my mind.

Really...how could you even suggest such a thing? I blush.

Howie


By this point, it is clear that Didi will be spending the night. I don't remember whether it's been discussed at length or if it's simply been assumed, but there is no issue. Saturday night there will certainly be a slumber party at my house.

For reasons that completely evade me – other than it feels like an amusing topic – I suggest a variety of sleeping arrangements. Although I'm convinced that there is only one place where she'll end up, I gallantly offer some other suggestions. This is a blatantly transparent – and completely unnecessary - guise to make her feel comfortable.

I detail the 3 potential sleeping locations in my apartment. The guestroom is upstairs. The sofa is on the main floor. And my own humble bed is downstairs. All of those possibilities, I suggest, are completely open to her.

We treat this discussion with infinitely more respect than it deserves.

Didi thinks that either the guestroom or the sofa will be fine. But the guestroom is really far away – so perhaps the sofa would be better. This is the "please don't go to any trouble on my account" position.

I am nauseatingly accommodating. The guest bed is more comfortable, but it's your choice. Sleep wherever you want.

Didi is most appreciative. But as she begins thinking out loud she eventually reaches a different conclusion. "Well, I'll probably stay on the sofa, but after awhile it will get lonely, and you'll have been so nice and you look so cute...I'll probably toss and turn for awhile and then come down to your bed."

It's not long afterwards that the inevitable conclusion is reached: we'll be in my bed. Imagine my surprise.

Somehow this amuses her. She re-traces the logic and her thinking. In point of fact, she has done ALL the talking and all of the thinking. I've been a passive bystander allowing her the freedom of choice. But she is pleased with her decision. She likes where it ended up, and she likes how it got there. For me, there was never a question.

But Didi does raise an interesting one:

*...not having done this before, i think someone needs to address a question we've been skirting – who's responsible for taking care of safe sex...what do we do?...who supplies the condoms?*


Miss D -

Fear not my queen. Options abound.

I have condoms.
I can pull out.
There's a reason why God invented mouths.
Nary an unsatisfactory solution in the lot.

H

The phone conversations continue. Without getting overly graphic, suffice it to say that Didi is very descriptive about what she likes having done to her and what she likes to do. She is a huge fan of oral sex.

Once again, I want to see where the discussion will go. How far it can go. So, I ask. And she's more than happy to grab the balls and run with them.

There is, of course, considerable discussion about how it will feel for her to lose her second virginity. How much she looks forward to that moment. And how wild, passionate and vocal she will be.

And there are, of course, questions. I wonder how she'll feel about the whole thing after so many years. Will she really be able to enjoy it? She wonders if I'll be man enough to handle a wild woman who will become liberated right before my eyes.

She tells me, with some pride, that she is a loud lover. I'm fine with that. My bedroom is a pretty quiet place – it will be nice to generate a little volume.

By now the phone calls have increased in both intensity and duration. If we talk for an hour, it's a short call. And, during the hour, the subject of sex is, essentially, the only topic.

As the date gets closer, natural concerns arise.

*howie........what a night!!.....i am up at this hour solely to work out.........i could not sleep thinking about meeting.........my cautious self kicked in with questions that were ridiculous, i.e.could he be the east side rapist?, i am staying with a man that i have no previous knowledge of, ad infinitum,......one of my close friends actually set that in motion yesterday......soooooooo, i just thought i would share later..........xxxxxx*

Miss D -

I know what you mean about not sleeping well. I've had the same problem - but for different reasons. It's difficult for me to sleep when I'm in a constant state of arousal.

I can understand your anxiety and I want to take it seriously. Frankly, I don't know how to put your concerns to rest. If I was a manipulative person, my guess is that I'd know the right things to calm you.

Here's one thought. Rape, as you know, is not a sexual act, it's an act of violence. It's hard to believe that, after all of our discussions, you could honestly believe that there is anything violent on my mind - the only thing I've been thinking about is the spectacular sexual experience that is awaiting both of us.

Rape is also an act of speed. Horrible though it may be, it is quick. We, on the other hand, we have experienced a full week of foreplay. It doesn't get any slower than that. On second thought, maybe it does. For you, a more accurate figure would actually be 7 years and one week.

Relax. I'm not the East Side Rapist. I'm not the Tribeca Rapist. But I do intend to eat you up.

Howie

By now, I now know the shape of her lips (the bottom one is large and full), what she likes to do with her tongue (pretty much everything) and the firmness of her nipples (extra firm when aroused).

For both of us, the mind has continued to race well into the night, long after the phones have been hung up. Because there is so much anticipation, so much sexual tension, sleep has become a prized commodity.

On Thursday night, we try to do something about it. She wants to move our conversation into a different arena. She wants us to have phone sex with the hope that a successful conclusion could at least help her sleep better.

I'm a willing participant, but frankly, pretty lame in my contributions. I don't know what to say and somehow just can't quite get into the flow. Viewed as an intellectual discussion, all the sex talk has been more than fine with me. But, moving into the verbal acrobatics of "baby, baby, oooh baby" has never been a lifelong desire.

Although I am essentially useless, Didi is willing to take full responsibility. She tells me what she is doing to herself, what she is feeling and what she is thinking as she masturbates. She warns me that when she has an orgasm, it will be loud.

Frankly, I'm not that worried. After all, I'm on the phone and miles away so no matter how much noise she makes, it won't bother me. I've had phone conversations with loud people before so I know what to do – just move the phone away from my ear. Frankly it ain't that complicated.

But moving the phone now is the last thing on my mind. I'm listening very closely. I pride myself on being a good listener. That ability comes in especially handy at this moment - especially as she begins to enter pre-climax mode. I'm listening. And I hear heavy breathing. Heavier breathing. Fast panting. And then... release.

Maybe because of the build-up, I was expecting more. Still, it's a pretty good show. After a few seconds of silence, Didi is willing to talk again. The abbreviated version: "Wow. I really needed that".

The next morning's email verified the experience.

*8 am*

*howie...........nice conversation last night and boy did i
sleep!!!.....i walked 2 miles this morning and hopefully,
weather permitting i will go do some laps later........ have
fun at your party.......try to be a good boy and not surround
yourself with a harem!!!!.......save your virtue for
me!!!........see you tomorrow............xxxx........me*

Excellent. Clearly, the concept of good sex followed by good
sleeping had been established. I, too, was looking forward
to a decent sleep – although my night of rest was still 2
days away.

On Friday, we have another discussion on the phone. One
good subject, and another, peculiar one.

Peculiar first. Didi had been kicked out of her gym that
morning. I never fully understand the reasons, but the issue
has something to do with Didi being loud and abusive to the
owner of the gym. It seems that Didi wanted to continue
arriving by 6 or 6:30 in the morning, but the owner didn't
want to open until later. An argument ensued and guess
who won? Didi was summarily given her money back and
told never to return.

I thought that was strange. Didi was obviously in a no-win
conversation. And, by being both angry and mean, she
obliterated any possibilities of getting her way. Still, she
bulled ahead and, predictably lost.

But she put it behind her relatively easily. She and her
girlfriend (could this possibly be my ménage partner?) had
decided to simply take their power walks early in the
morning and then join another local gym. It was a
reasonable solution. On the other hand, I never understood
the reason for the vitriol in the first place. Perhaps it was
still leftover angst from the cancelled Hollywood meeting.
Didi reported on the Thursday night dinner with her friends.
She was the hot topic of discussion. Everyone knew –

204

girlfriends, cousins, even out-of-towners - that on Saturday Didi was going to get laid. While all of them where happy for her (the phrases "finally" and "It's about time" were apparently repeated with regularity) some of them expressed concern. They weren't worried about Didi having sex. They were worried that she was going to have sex with someone she met – gasp! – on the internet. Some of them had read articles or seen frightening reports on TV. They worried that she her date might be with the East Side Rapist.

Frankly, I thought that the concern was reasonable. Although Didi and I had shared at least a dozen emails and considerably more hours on the phone, we were, in fact, strangers. I had no idea what she looked like. She may or may not have known what I looked like (eventually my photo did get posted on AOL – but by this time, I doubt whether she was referring to it anymore. After all, we were already knee-deep into infinitely more personal discussions).

In fact, in one of her emails, she had even touched on the subject of "Who are you anyway?" I took the issue seriously and tried to assuage her fears, but I also realized that they were grounded in reason. And, simply saying "I'm not an evil guy" just doesn't make the concern go away. When you think about it, there's almost nothing that can be said.

So her next email was not entirely unexpected.


*7 pm*

*howie............i am getting a case of "nerves"............here are my feelings and if i am off based, please let me know........#1-----what if i appear at your door and you decide that you do not like me?...................#2..........i have never done this before, where i jump in bed immediately with a great guy(you)!!!!........#3...........i*

205

*have visions of "one night stand" floating in my head.............#4...............i have such sexual longing for you coupled with the desire to learn more about you, but am i delusional?...........#5......i am currently blitzed from 2 glasses of wine(sic) and might be saying some things that might invoke this feeling you: fuck off little neophyte sex goddess!!!.......i am feeling a little woozy so i am going to recline horizontally at this time...........perhaps i am dreaming and tomorrow will never come.........ta ta............Didi (old siren of the silver screen)*

On the phone we discussed that email. Didi laughed it off. She insisted that she wasn't really concerned at all. She had brought up the topic as a joke. Even though we only knew each other by written word and by phone, she felt she definitely knew who I was. And she explained as much to her girlfriends. She was excited. She had absolutely no reservations at all.

That led to our last phone conversation on the eve of what was to be her second deflowering. We wondered what the elapsed time would be from the moment we first met until we were actually having sex.

I told her that once, for reasons that remain pretty surprising to me, I had a blind date that resulted in very early - almost immediate - sex. It had been a fix-up, so we both knew we were with safe people. And, we had been talking on the phone for about a week – although our conversations were neither as long nor as sexually explicit as the ones Didi and I had been enjoying. Still, for reasons that never were completely clear somehow, in about an hour, this woman and I were naked and in bed.

By most accounts, having sex an hour after first meeting is pretty damned fast. For me it was not just a record; no other experience even came close. Still, I told Didi that I was convinced we would easily beat the existing mark – probably by nearly an hour.

We agreed on an agenda: a hug, a glass of water, a pee (if necessary) and immediate sex. Assuming the necessity for all of them… total elapsed time from door to sack: 4 minutes, max.  3 was more probable.

Frankly, we didn't have much choice. After all the discussions and the build-up, the sexual tension leading up to our meeting would be so powerful, there would be only one way to release it. And it was a way we'd been discussing – endlessly – for a week.

We agreed that we didn't have to have great sex. That would surely come later. But we did need to have fast sex. Or, to be more accurate, immediate sex.

The idea amused us. Excited us. And, in many ways, seemed to be simultaneously both reasonable and preposterous. Add a third descriptor: inevitable.

When I awoke on Saturday morning, I checked the clock and mentally counted the hours. I'm not usually a morning person, but this morning I bounded out of bed. I was smiling already and nothing could wipe the grin off my face.

As I came upstairs to check the computer, I'm certain I wore the confident look of the soon-to-be well satisfied.

I knew the day's agenda. And I knew precisely how it would begin. Every day since our first email exchange, Didi sent me a "Good Morning" greeting. There was no question that today's greeting would be even more special.

It most certainly was.  Here it is:

*6 am*

*howie...........i have come to a conclusion and i just cannot go forward with this at this time.............i know that you will be angry and think that i am immature, but so be it.............where we go from here, i cannot say...........that is your decision*

I have recounted this sequence many times to many friends. Not a single one registered even the tiniest hint of surprise.

I, however, never anticipated that conclusion. In retrospect, I think it was only fitting. One way or another, I should have realized that the possibility of disappointment was inevitable. Reality has a nasty way of bursting fantasy balloons. And, for both of us, it was almost certainly better that the bubble busting didn't happen in person.

Although I was certainly disappointed at the time, as I view it now, this story ended the only way it possibly could. It's true that the destination was never reached but the journey was stimulating and memorable in every way.

# Oh yes I did

T.J. and I met at one of those events where singles on the hunt are supposed to mingle, exchange pleasantries, phone numbers, make plans to get together and eventually find love, happiness or something acceptably close.

I'm pretty sure that I was coaxed into attending this function by a friend who was fearful of being there alone and unguarded. He had good reason for concern – he is tall, handsome, successful, and because of that, has the equivalent of a blinking neon target affixed to his head at events such as these. I'm not sure why he felt that having a sidekick would lessen the attraction but going along for the ride was a non-decision for me. I'd happily take his leftovers.

While all of the other women were there to meet men, T.J. was there to meet men and women. That's not because she is bi-sexual (although there is no specific reason to rule out that possibility). She was there on business. I don't know what her former occupation was but she had recently joined the matchmaking "profession". She had established herself as the sole proprietor of a fledging enterprise in an industry that has a long and storied history but was only recently bringing in the big bucks. In other words, while pretty much everyone else was looking for love, T.J. was working the room to line up people who invariably needed an assist in their pursuits.

Her sales pitch was pretty straightforward. The one thing that successful people don't seem to have is time. They're busy working, making deals, volunteering and being pillars of the community. How, with so much going on in their life, can they possibly allocate the time needed to find the one magical person to share their hopes, dreams, values and rent controlled apartment?

Well, that was the story she fed them. The truth is that many clients of matchmakers (OK, practically all of them) are socially inept. Some have been single for life because they have never been able to consummate a successful relationship. Some are divorced for precisely the same reason. All, apparently, are susceptible to the "it's not your fault" strategy.

So here was T.J. in a room filled with ripe prospects. Like a mosquito in a nudist colony, she barely knew where to start.

When she and I began a conversation, she was reluctant to reveal her true mission. Just as there are ethics among thieves, apparently the hosts of the "get-acquainted-make-a-connection" events frown upon having their venue used as fodder for similar purposes. Although this was hardly amateur hour, the "no professionals allowed" rule was, if not strictly enforced, understood and agreed upon.

With a knowing smile, T.J. told me that she couldn't tell me what her job was. Which, as should be obvious, made it impossible for me not to set up a date so I could uncover her mysterious occupation.

And so the relationship - such as it was - began. We waffled between tepid and torrid, seeing each other occasionally but definitely not exclusively. Our conversations were easy, although hardly deep and often bordering on meaningless. But as most single folk know all too well, sometimes you have a choice between being alone or spending the evening with someone you're at least somewhat comfortable with. That's pretty much the way we both saw it. Sometimes she called me; sometimes I called her. Often we went for weeks without seeing or talking to each other. When we did get together there was some kissing and some foreplay but we never got to endgame status. It was a Friends Without Benefits relationship.

Until...

It had been awhile. No calls. No communication. And, for both of us, that seemed to be just fine. Then we bumped into each other at a place neither of us usually frequented. Maybe it was because the meeting was unexpected, maybe it was because we missed each other or maybe the stars were appropriately aligned. But whatever the reason, we both had an extremely positive reaction.


It was early afternoon on a Friday. T.J. was just finishing lunch with a friend when I arrived at the restaurant after an all-nighter in preparation for an early morning client presentation. I don't recall the client, the topic or the result of that morning meeting but I do know that when it was over, I needed two things: food and sleep.

At the restaurant, relatively meaningless chitchat ensued even though I was barely able to keep up my end of the chatter. I was able, however, to suggest that after a much-needed nap, perhaps we could get together for dinner, a film or whatever. (Even in my sleep-deprived state, I was sufficiently coherent to hope for "whatever").

There are some days – wonderful, dreamy days - when there is precious little that is more delicious than an afternoon nap. The bed seems especially comfortable, troubles evaporate into thin air and hours melt away in peaceful slumber. There are other days, however, when no matter the level of exhaustion, sleep simply will not come. The room is too hot or too cold, tired legs are too exhausted to relax or the mind won't stop racing even though it hasn't a clue where it's headed.

That day, despite best intentions, there would be no rest for Howie. I honestly did try to sleep but failed miserably. About the only accomplishment I can claim is that I took a long, hot shower and remembered to wash behind my ears.

In the parlance of film, this is commonly known as "cutting to the chase." T.J. and I wound up at her apartment.

But first, a quick diversion.

There's an old joke about a moderator who asks the crowd for a show of hands. He asks, "how many of you have sex more than twice a week?" Several people smile broadly and raise their hands. "How many have sex once a week?" Many more hands raise and there are many more smiles. "How many have sex once a month?" Sheepishly, a few hands slowly go up but the faces are dour. "How many have sex only once a year?" One guy stands, grinning from ear to ear and waves his hand wildly. The moderator is understandably perplexed so the he asks the only reasonable question, "if you only have sex once a year, why are you so happy?" The guy gleefully blurts out: "tonight's the night!"

Back to the story. For reasons that are not important and, even if they were, need not be explained, somehow, like the guy in the joke, we both knew that tonight was the night.

We began kissing in the living room, standing by the window. Eventually we made our way to the sofa. From there, progress continued in the usual manner. Articles of clothing were removed in sequence and carelessly strewn on the floor. Kissing continued. Eventually, the line that we had not crossed before was traversed.

There is no other way to say it: we had sex.

It's important that I make this clear: I'm not proud of what happened. It's not something I like to talk about. It's not something I'd want carved on my gravestone. And it's absolutely why T.J. isn't her real name.

I fell asleep.

To be fair, it's well known that the release of testosterone is proven to promote sleep. That's why many men often nod off shortly after having sex.

But that isn't what happened. I didn't fall asleep afterwards. I fell asleep *during*.

I think reasonable people would agree that my timing was less than propitious. And, though I may have slept for only a moment or two - even if it was the fastest power nap in world history - there are undoubtedly far better times for me to have caught up on my rest.

It's true that I was exhausted. It's also true that, at the moment, I was experiencing many of the feelings that make sleep so irresistible – comfort, satisfaction and pleasure. So I do have excuses. None, however, are acceptable.


For obvious reasons, T.J. and I did not speak again and, fortunately for both of us, our paths never crossed. My guess is that she is as reluctant as I am to share this story.

I do not carry the memory as a badge of honor even though my actions make me a member of a very select group.

I may be one of the very few people who can claim to have fucked and fucked up at precisely the same time.

# The Horny Widow

The recommendation came from the friend of a friend. Essentially the initial information was brief. It was something like, "you need to meet the Widow Berman."

Later on, additional facts were added – the most enticing was the specific indication that she was lonely and very much looking forward to getting laid.

Armed with that insight, there were definite questions that I should have asked. For example, it might have been worthwhile to have at least some indication of why the widow was lonely. Was she unattractive? Unlovable? Unlikeable? Annoying? Boorish? Overbearing? Disfigured? Lacking some important but noticeable body parts?

I might also have questioned her unrealized craving for coupling. Quite often men who desire sexual fulfillment are rejected or are so intimidated by the fear of rejection that they end up where they began – alone and unsatisfied. But a woman who wants sex seems far less likely to have her bed remain unshared. The answer to the question, "excuse me sir but would you mind having sex with me?" is highly likely to be in the affirmative.

But I didn't ask those questions. Even though I had only recently met this friend of a friend, he seemed like a stand-up guy. And, what he was offering was undeniably tempting. So, when he called to give me her phone number, I wrote it down and, within a few days, dialed it.

A lot is revealed in a phone conversation and the information that gets communicated goes far beyond the topics that are discussed. Voice quality, sense of humor, intelligence, attitude and the ability to listen are all revealed within minutes. Although I didn't really have much of a test in mind, The Widow Berman easily passed. She was unquestionably bright, caustic, sarcastic, and, true to what I had been told, interested in having her horns trimmed.

Too much information too soon? Too much information for a first phone call? Well, yes. But I wasn't complaining. It's what I signed up for and it was nice to have confirmation.

There was another thing that piqued my interest: her address. She not only lived on the Upper East Side but on 5$^{th}$ avenue in a very high toned location. It was almost certainly a doorman building and definitely much more formal than my own downtown digs. Just getting to see her apartment would be worth the price of admission. And oh, there was also the getting laid thing.

During a short, second phone conversation the details were set. We'd meet at her place, have dinner and sometime before, after or during, satisfy some carnal desires.

I feel the need to explain that I'm really not that kind of guy. This whole episode was totally out of character. Opportunities like this have not been a significant part of my history. Which is not to say that I wasn't game for the experience. I was happily all-in. While it would be correct to say that I'm usually not that easy, that would be difficult to prove. Opportunities like this one are not, for me, a regular occurrence. In almost every way, this was a first.

Cutting to the chase...

I get to her building and it's just as posh I expected. It's not only on 5$^{th}$ avenue; it's located directly across from the park. As anticipated, there is a doorman and, pretty much as anticipated, there are elevator buttons for a lot of floors - 22 in all. There is an additional button for the penthouse – and that's where she resides.

I'm definitely impressed. I'm even more impressed when I see the apartment. It's not just the penthouse; it's a two-story penthouse with balconies that encircle the entire building on both floors. In the realm of great New York City apartments, this one is not an "A". It's unquestionably an "A+".

The tour takes about 20 minutes. And that's just the nickel tour. You know the drill - it's the "this is the living room, this is the dining room, this is the office" tour. There are some unavoidable stories about the famous person who got drunk in this room and is never going to be invited here again. And, of course, there are the memorable-to-her but boring-to-me origins of some of the art and furniture.

Whether by design, happy accident or simply because of the way the apartment is laid out, the master bedroom is where the tour culminates. Like the rest of the place, the bedroom is spacious and ineptly decorated with plenty of furniture and very little sense of style. All of the appropriate dressers, lamps and tables are represented. None seem to have any visual relationship to any of the others.

But this doesn't seem to be the time to discuss interior design or the lack thereof. There are other issues to be dealt with. The timing is right, the location is right and yet there is hesitation. Not from her. From me.

I came here with a specific purpose in mind. Our phone conversations were hardly bathed in subtlety or innuendo. The evening's agenda could not have been more specific. And yet, at the precise moment when action is required, I'm just not quite ready.

We've all see films where the moment has arrived when we are about to witness the heavy petting inevitably escalate into something rated X, XX or even X-ier. But then, much to our dismay, the guy suddenly finds himself in touch with his higher moral self and leaves the woman – as well us all of us in the audience – unfulfilled.

At that moment, we are all more than disappointed. We're confused. What's the hold-up? She is beautiful, willing and more than ready. But for reasons that are incomprehensible to us, he has chosen to do what he believes to be the honorable thing, which is to do nothing except leave.

What is he thinking? And why did we fork over the price of admission if we're not going to get our money's worth?

In this particular instance, the situation is more than slightly different. The three variables – beautiful, willing and ready – are not all entirely applicable. To be specific, "beautiful" would be considered by most, to be more than a stretch.

She is definitely present. She is definitely willing. But beautiful? Not so much.

How much less than a raving beauty is she? Well, later, whenever I relate this saga to friends, I explain the widow Berman thusly – "she looks like a short, fat, ugly man."

That description is, of course, somewhat of an exaggeration. But not, however, entirely incorrect. She does possess the necessary parts to prove that she is indeed a woman but there is nothing alluring, appealing or even slightly enticing about the way those parts have been assembled.

A better man than I might have been able to come up with an excuse for not sampling her wares. A faster thinking man might even have come up with an explanation quickly enough to bow out gracefully. And any reasonable man would have had enough sense to bolt for the exit with or without a word of goodbye.

Not me.

Against my better or even lesser judgment I took the "grin and bear it" approach and, with full misgivings, continued on the path that usually leads to satisfaction. But there wasn't a second when I didn't know full well that this time it would lead nowhere close.

We went through the motions in the normal order. Apparel was discarded and coupling began. The consummate act didn't take long and the result, not unexpectedly, fell considerably short of total bliss. But the deed was definitely done. And for me, a new record has been set. From first meeting at the front door, to having sex, to getting dressed and leaving for the restaurant, not even an hour has elapsed. I've had shorter naps. And, frankly, the shorter naps were more satisfying.

The rest of the evening was sheer torment. I'd given in to the most base, the most prurient of instincts and now I had to pay the price. It wasn't the cost of the meal that concerned me. It was how I was going to get through the next few hours.

Although I counted the minutes until I could reasonably make my escape, Ms. Berman was having a wonderful time. She didn't notice that the sex was deplorable – for her it may well have been all she hoped it would be. So, while I did my best not to keep my sulking from being too obvious, she was smiling, chatting and explaining how she looked forward to our post dinner rendezvous as soon as we got back to her bedroom.

It never happened. I don't remember what excuse I came up with but I must have been convincing or at least insistent because I was able to make my getaway without re-entering either her or her apartment.

Once was more than enough. Returning for sloppy seconds was never a consideration. There are some things even a fabulous penthouse apartment in Manhattan simply can't overcome.

# Gently Fade to Black

Most stories – and certainly all of the good ones – have a beginning, middle and end.

This one has those bases covered – albeit not particularly well. Just as in baseball, merely reaching first, second and third doesn't count as a score.

For Regina and me, the beginning was unsurprising. The end came not with a bang and barely even a faint whimper. The middle, although pleasant enough, lacked any snap, crackle or pop.

Not all potential relationships that fail to live up to potential are fueled with drama, tension or passion. Sometimes they just don't work. The high notes aren't particularly high. The electricity doesn't jolt. And even though the gears ought to mesh, the engine never quite revs up to speed.

There were mitigating factors. Timing definitely worked against us. Shortly after we began to correspond, 9/11 happened. And, because my apartment was deep in the heart of Ground Zero, I was, to say the least, enormously distracted.

I spent well over a month as a displaced person– living almost the entire time in a Westside apartment owned by friends. Their apartment is beautiful and I had it all to myself because they were in France. Knowing what many of my friends and neighbors were dealing with made it ridiculous for me to complain about my posh surroundings. Still, it wasn't my house, it wasn't my computer and, like most of the residents of downtown Manhattan, I was way off of my game.

My inability to focus was hardly surprising because my apartment was about 4 blocks from Ground Zero. I was home when the planes hit, when the towers fell and when the ground shook like a 6.0 earthquake. For unaccountable reasons, my phone service was uninterrupted and throughout the day I fielded calls from concerned friends all across America. Late in the afternoon I was visited by police who told me I had to evacuate.

For all of the obvious reasons, it was less than an opportune time for a budding a relationship. While that may be an acceptable excuse, thinking back now, it's hard to say whether 9/11 was just another justification for the fizzle.

Regina and I maintained communication either by phone or email on a fairly regular basis. We went out several times, had dinner at each other's apartments and heard music at a few jazz clubs. Everything was good. Everything was fine. Nothing was great.

For many reasons, it's important – at least to me - to establish that Regina is undeniably terrific – attractive, smart, easy to be with and by any fair evaluation, a thoroughly good person. All the boxes were properly checked. There was no fatal flaw. There was simply a lack of magic.

So our story is really a non-story. Perhaps that's often the case. The arc of romance doesn't always race to heights or plummet to earth in free fall. Regina and I didn't crash and burn. We just eased in and slid out.

It all started with an email from her:
\

*So you enjoy going to jazz clubs, off-broadway, flea markets AND dance performances? A winning combination in my estimation.*

*I don't have a profile set up but if I did it would look something like this...*

*I am 51, never married, 5' 2", white, raised Jewish but don't practice, educated (Masters). My income is large enough that I am able to go to the clubs, theater and dance (I save at the fleas). I like a scotch before dinner and a glass of good wine with. I exercise enough so I can drink what I like, although... well... I am 51.*

*I am a huge jazz fan a la Monk, Brubeck, Evans, Cannonball Adderley, Miles -- you'd be listening to any one of them if you were visiting me at home. Going to the clubs is one of my favorite things to do—and this is the primary reason why your profile got my attention. I don't meet many who have the same taste in music. My favorite clubs are the Vanguard and the Jazz Standard and I'm partial to really good piano jazz -- Fred Hersch and Bill Charlap are two I've heard recently.*

*I've been studying piano too for a couple of years now – mostly classical, some jazz -- I've gotten past the notion that I'll ever make it to the major leagues but it gives me great pleasure to play for myself.*

*I am very much a city girl but can be a country one too... just returned from a trip to the Mt Hood National Forest in Oregon -- stunning country and excellent hiking. But I'm the sort of hiker that looks forward to the hot shower, cocktail and dinner at the hotel after a long day on the trails.*

*What else? I am a consultant/trainer for an online information services provider -- I'm home-based but spend most of my days traveling around the city visiting clients. Challenging and rewarding work....*

*Need more encouragement? I will gladly send a photo.*

*Cheers -*
*Regina*

**Note:**

It's easy to understand why I responded so quickly and why, just as quickly, we began a back and forth email exchange that was light, easy and held promise of good things to come.


Hi Regina -

Well, you certainly saw my Monk, Miles and Brubeck and raised me a whole bunch. I'm not familiar with either Fred Hersch or Bill Charlap. But I've found that often when I go to hear live jazz the musicians are unknown to me. Nevertheless, not only have I seldom been disappointed, I invariably leave quite impressed.

The Vanguard is one of my favorite places, although lately I've gone to Smoke (it's pretty far up on the West Side). The Standard is good, too, but it is a bit larger than the other clubs. One of the things I like best about hearing the music live is being so close to the players. I find it completely electrifying.

One of my sons is now playing progressive jazz - but his music is a little too inaccessible for me. Many of the musicians he's playing with are extremely talented and sometimes when they lock into a grove, I'm right with them. But then they move on to non-melodic, discordant, complex rhythms and sounds, and I'm totally lost.

I'll be glad to join you for the wine, but I may have to pass on the Scotch. Not that I have anything against drinking - it's just that I never quite developed a taste for that particular beverage. Usually, if I do the hard stuff, it's usually bourbon. Although, I must admit, the single malts do hold some appeal.

Yes, of course, I'd love to see a photo. It's never a deal breaker or a deal maker, but for some reason, it is part of the mix. And, for good or ill, you have seen mine.

I look forward to hearing from you.

Howie


*Hi Howie:*

*So your son is a musician? What instrument? I know what you mean about the progressive stuff... I find it difficult to listen to as well. I wandered into Smoke one eve for just a minute-- looked like a nice play to spend some time – I didn't particularly like the sax I was hearing so didn't stay very long.*

*Enough about jazz... except... do you read The New Yorker? There was a very sweet article about Bill Evans in the 8/13 issue... about a recording he did 40 years ago. You might like to read it.*

*On to flea markets, etc. I expect you go to 26th street? Ever been to Lambertville or Stormville? Do you collect something? I don't collect but enjoy wandering through just looking. But I did have a very good time buying when I was furnishing my apartment.*

*Are you originally from California? I lived out there myself for about 10 years and then came to my senses and returned to NY. I was in San Diego – a beautiful place but it's just not New York.*

*Hope you get the .jpg file to load okay... and that you like what you see.*

*Regina*

Hi Miss R -

Lots of questions. Some answers.

My son plays bass. Not stand-up; electric. For a long time, as a kid, he was heavily into rock and roll so it was understandable that he became a strictly metal guy. Frankly, I liked it all. I understood it, could follow the beat, and enjoyed the performance. Now, I only go to some of his shows and often feel completely out of sync with the extremely progressive jazz that's being played.

Of course I've done the 26th street flea markets, although they've changed considerably over the last year. With the new buildings going up, the 2 biggest ones are gone and the one across the street isn't nearly as good as the others used to be. I've also been to Lambertville. I have good friends who live in Carversville - about 10 miles from New Hope - so a visit to Lambertville is almost a given. A hundred years ago, I was a counselor in a camp in Stormville, but I wasn't aware of the flea market scene there.

I find that my attitude about the fleas is quite different than it used to be. Prices now have soared and take much of the fun out of the process. People have no idea what they're selling but have no problem putting ridiculous prices on it. Most of my visits now are just for browsing - I seldom buy anything anymore.

My only real collection is cookie jars. I bought most of them for under $5 - a price that doesn't get much of anything these days. When people are charging hundreds for a cookie jar, what's the point and where's the fun? The whole idea of a flea market, I think, is to uncover a bargain. Obviously, I'm out of step with what's going on now. So, I go to look around, be outside, and treat the process much like a visit to a museum.

I lived in LA for nearly 20 years – most of the time right under the Hollywood sign. Loved every minute of it - but now have no desire to return. I used to return fairly often to shoot commercials, but the more I went, bck the less I liked it.

I did get your jpeg, but either due to my own ineptitude or my computer, haven't been able to open it. Frankly, it's not an issue at all. My feeling is that if we get to spend an evening listening to jazz together, there's no downside.

My own schedule is a little nuts for the rest of the month. I'm out of town this coming weekend for a wedding in upstate NY, and the following Friday I leave for Chicago and San Diego and won't be back until after Labor Day. But my guess is that there will still be live music being played in September. If you're around, we can surely find a way to get together.

Howie


*Howie –*

*Sorry about the photo but I appreciate your willingness to not let it become a major issue.*

*For what it's worth, I was 'hit on' by a 26 year old at Barnes & Noble this evening.  No, he didn't think I was in my '20's--- apparently has a thing for older women-- but it was flattering (and a bit shocking) nevertheless.*

*I'll be out of town myself for a few days around Labor Day. I'll be in Sarasota for a visit with a friend and then Orlando on business.  Back after the 5th. I'll look forward to getting together with you some time after that.*

*Best-*
*Regina*

Regina -

Congratulations on the pick-up attempt at Barnes & Noble. Just because the guy says he has a thing for older women doesn't necessarily mean he thinks you're more than 30. At 26, an older woman is anyone older than 27.

So, let's say we have a plan. Early in Sept. we'll start checking the jazz scene in town and find a show that seems interesting. And, if we can't come up with anything special, we'll just go to the Vanguard and hear whoever is playing. Every time I've done that, I've always come away impressed.

Howie


*You are a very funny person Howie - but then you already knew that.*
*'Til September then... happy travels*

*Regina*




**Note:**

From this point on, things got a bit fuzzy. I can't locate my emails to her. But there's a good reason. Once the 9/11 happened, everything was up for grabs.

All of the residents in my building were forced to leave. Most of them ended up in hotel rooms. I was much more fortunate. For about a month I luxuriated in my friends' apartment. My accommodations were great so, compared to the others, I didn't have that issue to complain about. But everything else - for me and for them - was turned upside down.

The enormity of the event was inconceivable. It was the only thing any of us could talk about for weeks on end. Everyone had stories – where they were when the towers fell, how they got home, how they located their friends and, most of all, what that meant for all of us in America.

When I left my apartment, I brought almost nothing with me. I didn't have time or the mental clarity to think about packing a suitcase. At most, I may have brought a toothbrush and shirt. After a few days, I was able to get back into my loft to pick up some clothes and other necessities. That visit and all subsequent ones required a military escort and often someone from the police department as well.

When people say that downtown Manhattan during that time was like a war zone, they're wrong. It <u>was</u> a war zone. Military equipment lined both sides of every street, the only people present were either police or U.S. Army and, although there was no fighting or gunshots, any pretense of normalcy was impossible.

What I remember most about that time was the awful smell. It was unlike any odor I'd experienced before and hopefully one that I'll never know again. Difficult to describe, it was an intense mixture of everything that had been destroyed or burned – concrete, metal, plastic and, sadly, people.

The stench was everywhere. Subways were closed, but even months later when the trains began to run, the odor was still pervasive. The smell permeated everything - the buildings, apartments and even the subway stations below ground. It took months to eventually fade away but, because the sense of smell is stronger than any other memory, this is one that is impossible to forget.

Communicating with anyone during that time was difficult at best. I was able to locate some of Regina's emails but certainly not all. And the ones I've found are surely out of sequence. Neither the loss of my emails or the misplacement of hers is a tragedy because, even though we did our best to keep things light, the humor quotient, heavily influenced by all that surrounded us, was not particularly high.

Somehow after the Towers fell, even in the midst of the chaos, Regina and I were able to get together a few times. Downtown was almost completely closed down but further north things were surprisingly normal. Restaurants and clubs functioned as if the tragedy had occurred in another state and not a mere few blocks away.

We listened to live music, ate out, wandered the city streets and pretended that all was fine even though nothing actually was. Somehow, despite shared interests and some physical attraction, our relationship never materialized; never gelled. Everything was fine; nothing was great. Although it is tempting to put the blame on the unusual circumstances and difficult timing, I'm not sure that's the reason. Sometimes people are not meant to be together. The stars just never seem to align.

There was no dramatic ending, no tears, no fighting and no promises – false or otherwise. I'm pretty sure that we didn't even talk about the fact that it was over. The demise was simply understood.

Whatever we had didn't end with a thud. Just a slow, gentle fadeout.

# Great Expectations.  Unrealized.

Spoiler alert: this is not going to end well. But maybe the title gave that away.

So you have several choices.

If you're looking for a happy ending you can stop now. (No points will be deducted for early drop-outs).

You can skip directly to the end to find out how things fell apart. You will, of course, miss the much of the verbal foreplay but need not worry because none of that will be included on the final exam.

Or you can follow along as the story unfolds and try to guess something neither of the participants anticipated - where, when and how everything unravels.

As is typical in cyberspace relationships, this story begins with emails. Mona's first:

*Wow, you sound refreshingly wonderful. Sending pix if interested give me a buzz and I'll write you many paragraphs.*

*Mona*

The "pix" that Mona sent was terrific. It was just a head and shoulders shot - not sexy, not alluring, not inappropriate. She was way beyond cute - all the way up to very, very pretty with short blonde hair and a lovely smile. Although I had a long-stated commitment to only two requirements for the woman I was searching for (those requirements being "smart" and "funny"), like most men, I'm a sucker for beautiful.

There was no chance that I wouldn't respond.

Hi Mona -

If I had a photo that looked as good as yours, I wouldn't feel the need to say anything in my Profile. You look sensational.

You already know a little about me. I'd love to know more about you.

Howie

*Okay Howie here goes- Glad you liked my pix now let's see if I can work up some interest in the real woman. I'm div. two grown fabulous kids two small delicious grandchildren. I own a small but thriving real estate business in Bayside Queens. I live in Great Neck, a very affluent Jewish community of which I am neither. I really have a pretty cool life now- Great family life- love running my business and a really full social life. Of course what's missing is that one special intimate relationship that really completes the pix. I have a pretty outgoing personality and I am kinda smart and kinda funny (at least so I've been told) I'm very drawn to interesting creative people and am definitely the best audience in the world. I've been on AOL 4 mos and have met my fair share of men but not the counterpart that I'm looking for. Although I can be traditional in some things I'm also drawn to the outrageous. I like to hit the high notes. Everything you mentioned I enjoyed except we definitely do not have the same taste in music. I'm a classic rock n rock nut but love music so much I'm open to being exposed to anything. I adore coming into manhattan. Grew up in Bethlehem, PA and am forever in awe that I have this unbelievable city to play in. I answered your ad because beside being kind of cute you were interesting and different and definitely not run of the mill. So that's it for now. Enjoy your day and hope to hear from you.*

*Mona*

Miss M -

Well...you did good. Lots of information and all of it positive.

Why is your business in Bayside when you live in Great Neck? I don't know much about NY geography, but I happen to have a tiny bit of knowledge about those two places - and they seem pretty disparate. When I was a counselor in camp a hundred years ago, my girlfriend lived in Great Neck. In my mind, she is still 20 years old and beautiful. I don't think I need to see her now and have my vision dashed. Great Neck seemed pretty nice at the time. But Bayside? Well, if the business is thriving, I guess there's no reason to question it.

You've had more experience with AOL than I have. My Profile has been up for about 2 weeks and while there have been quite a few responses; my interest level in most of the women has been pretty minimal. When they describe themselves as being "full figured" even I understand the euphemism. I'm not usually attracted to heavy women but I'm all too familiar with the other problem. My ex-wife was both anorexic and bulimic. Either extreme can be very sad.

I guess I'm a pretty committed city boy. I have a loft in Tribeca. So not only am I into the city, I'm into the downtown part as well.

I was glad to hear that you like to come to New York. But frankly, you really haven't missed much these past few days. When the city gets hot, more than the temperature is problematic. Not only do tempers rise but so do the aromas that waft through the street. The only safety is hiding indoors and cranking the air conditioning.

Hope you're beating the heat in Great Neck.

Howie

Howie,

I'll begin by answering your questions. My business is in Bayside because the type of real estate I do only works in Bayside.I specialize in renting apartments. We are only a 20 min. train ride from Manhattan and are loaded with 2 family houses so it's truly a wonderful area.  When I opened my business 7 years ago I was in a very desperate financial situation. Separated and really not supporting myself well. There was nothing in Bayside that specialized in Rentals and my son and I took a shot on this and lo and behold it took off.  It was really a godsend for me. Not only did it support me but I really found my niche. But although I'm committed to my business I really have plenty of free time. You know the well-oiled machine thing. So while everyone around me is talking of retirement I'm only climbing the ladder. But wouldn't have it any other way. Now as for the other issue. My dream is to find a lover in Manhattan. Don't get scared now. If I could be in the city every night I would be. The typical suburban attitude about coming into Manhattan is so not mine. Drive in at the drop of a hat as they say.

Believe me its as hot out here as where you are. Actually I have a few friends in the Hamptons I spoke to this week and it's even hot by the beach. I tolerate the heat very well. I'm Bethlehem tough. I think I mentioned I had my 85 yr. old mom up here this week.  Just put her on the plane wed. She was fighting with me about  putting on the ac . I really only have the bedroom and den air conditioned because I have a really large airy apartment and I couldn't bear to have it sealed up. Anyway on the hottest day she was making us pasta for dinner and there we sat in 95 degrees eating linguine. You try arguing with an 85 yr. old tough little Italian lady.

I am a bit of a movie fanatic. I will travel to most art cinemas to see the latest cool films and cannot believe these last 2 weeks I have seen 3 of the goofiest summer movies out. Saw Rush hour 2 with Charlie from my office *because we wanted a reprieve from the heat. Saw Diary of a Princess because I had to get away for a few hours to collect myself last week and was with every little girl in Great Neck. And I saw Legally Blonde last night because I met my girlfriend for dinner and she begged me. I feel like I've been eating cotton candy for a week. Of the three Legally Blonde was actually adorable. Reese Witherspoon is winsome enough to hold your attention. As for the rest I can only say the theater was really nicely air conditioned.*

*What do you do on the week-end in Tribeca.? Are you a beach person at all? My dearest friend has a beautiful house in Amangansett and our crowd hangs out in for a major portion of the weekends in July and August. It's just so beautiful there. We love to party and cook and just enjoy the area and each other.*

*Enjoy and hope to hear back from you*
*.*
*Mona*

*I'm still kind of hopeless on this computer and cannot go back and correct my spelling mistakes so please forgive and truly understand that I am literate.*

Hi Mona -

Good to hear from you.

I understand (and share) the difficulties with computers - so there's no need to apologize. You do sound quite literate, quite ambitious, and quite successful. Most impressive.

Starting your own business and making it work is an extraordinary accomplishment. The fact that you have built the machine so it can run without your daily presence is even more impressive. And the best part is that you're looking to expand. Onward and upward. You go girl.

Although you wrote a lot (that's not a criticism. In fact it's quite the opposite - I truly appreciate the time you spent writing to me) you did drop a little bombshell smack in the middle. And I want you to know that it caught my attention - big time.

Here's what you said: "My dream is to find a lover in Manhattan. Don't get scared now. If I could be in the city every night I would be. The typical suburban attitude about coming into Manhattan is so not mine. In fact I've looked for men in the city on computer and have met quite a few of them. Drive in at the drop of a hat as they say".

I can promise you, I didn't get scared. Excited, yes. Interested, yes. Thinking about getting together, yes.

So, if a hat happened to drop - say, this Sunday - do you think you could make it into the city?

As to the other things you wrote about: I'm not as willing as you are to take in a movie in order to escape the heat. There are lots of air conditioned places that make me much happier. Seeing a film is certainly something we could consider doing on Sunday - although there are probably better places for us to get acquainted.

I know what you mean about the inability to handle an aging mother. Mine is a little bull, and once she takes a position, she's hard to move - physically, emotionally, or rationally. Sometimes I think that can be amusing - although I'm not sure that I would have been able to eat pasta - even really great homemade pasta - in a 95 degree kitchen.

Let me know what you think about Sunday.

Howie

*Howie,*

*Oh wow I hope I didn't come across too forward. I did say Lover didn't I?? Of course I meant after a proper time. Oh single life is so complex. Too sexual is scary and too puritanical is off setting. But I'm sure you're cool enough to figure it out. Or figure me out. Anyway I would love to get together Sunday if you can arrange it. I would have a little rearranging to do but it could be done easily if you give me a little notice.*

*Did I give you my phone nos. Can't remember so here goes. home 000-000-0000 work 000-000-0000. Can find me at either place most of tomorrow. Hope we can work it out you sound delicious.*

*Mona*

(Two quick e-mails follow up emails from Mona)

1.

*Do you like to dance?????????*

A brief one arrived a little bit later

2.

*Just reread your profile and had overlooked your comment on dancing. So you'll watch me. Went out with some friends to a large club on Long Island last night and can really got into it. The club was loud and rocking and everybody was high just on the music.*

*Enjoyed talking to you and really looking forward to meeting. You were as interesting and bright and funny as your profile promised. Coming into Manhattan tonite actually to have dinner somewhere on the upper east side.*

*You have a loft i read. very cool. Have to take a look at that. Pick a place for dinner close to your place and maybe we can sneak a look at your digs. speak to you.*

*Mona*


Mona -

Don't be concerned about the dancing. Depending on the mood, the situation, and who I'm with, I can enjoy being a participant too. A big club with lots of people having a good time is hard to resist.

No problem finding a restaurant close to my loft. There must be at least 50 good ones within a 5-block radius. I haven't made a reservation yet, but I'll take care of that very soon.

Howie


*Howie,*

*Came home to write you in this torrential downpour. WHATS WITH THE WEATHER. ARE WE IN OZ.//////?????? Anyway I have a little scheduling problem. I had a company picnic scheduled for tomorrow night and the whole office begged me to change it till wednesday because the weather is a little threatening for tomorrow. SO can we change the evening. I'm free tomorrow night or thurs. Either one of those work for you?? hope so. I will be home tonite after 8 so call me or write me. Hope wherever you are you're dry because I look like a drowned kitten after running thru this storm.*

*Stay dry.*
*Mona*
Hi Mona -

Sorry about the weather - I'm doing the best I can. But I can't work with this constant complaining. First it was the heat, then it was the humidity, and now it's the rain. I've given you air conditioning and umbrellas - what more do you want from me?

And, just between us girls, I'm kinda into the drowned kitty look. At least it's a statement.

On the other hand, I find it hard to believe that you feel that your entire staff, all your business associates, and your future business could actually be more important than having dinner with me. Imagine...after all we've meant to each other. Where are your values? And how do you plan on making up for the overwhelming sense of rejection? I'm hopeful that you'll find a way.

I'll call tonight and we'll make alternate plans.

Howie


**Note:**

We made alternate plans. By this time it was almost past the time when we should have met in person. And it was pretty clear that the lead-up was pretty enticing for both of us. We'd been communicating by phone and email for quite awhile – certainly enough to pique interests.

I think we were both optimistic. I was certainly impressed that she started her own business and made it a success. That's quite an accomplishment under any circumstances but beginning with no financial reserves and no experience in the field made it even more impressive.

And of course her photo kicked it up a notch. She was very pretty. Very.

There was obviously some appeal for her as well. Our conversations – both online and on the phone – were light and easy and the fact that I had a downtown loft definitely impressed her.

So the hopes for our first get together were high. As it turned out, unrealistically so.

Although Mona had told me that the city was only a 20-minute train ride away, she decided to drive instead. Under normal conditions, Great Neck is probably an hour away. With traffic, it's anyone's guess. And, given the torrential downpour that evening, it was destined to be a long, long ride.

Close to an hour after she began the journey, Mona called from her car. The situation was hopeless. Because of the rain, traffic was a mess and there was no way she'd be able to make it in time for our dinner reservation. She was frustrated, upset and only called to tell me that she had decided to turn back.

I don't remember the specifics of the conversation but I have no doubt that at least some of the discussion included:

1. Letting her know that calling an audible would be easy. Dinner reservations can be cancelled and ordering out in downtown Manhattan limits the choices to only about 100 restaurants.

2. We'd both been looking forward to the evening so not getting together would be a big disappointment. And since she was already more than halfway here, why not complete the journey?

So, despite her better judgment, she pressed on. Not surprisingly, the rest of her trip didn't go well. Traffic continued to snarl, the rain continued to pelt, Mona got lost and even after she finally found my place, she had trouble finding parking. When she arrived she was drenched, tense, and hardly in the best of spirits.

I, on the other hand, had no reason to complain. After all, I wasn't the one driving in a downpour. I wasn't the one dealing with miserable traffic. And I wasn't the one heading towards an unfamiliar and overcrowded part of Manhattan.

For me, waiting in my comfortable apartment only increased the anticipation. I was in good spirits, thoroughly willing and fully intent on being an understanding and, at the very least, welcoming and generous host.

For Mona, the evening was already hopeless. I got the same feeling when I opened the door and unexpectedly found myself face to face with someone who looked nothing like the ravishing beauty I had seen in photos.

The issue of what to include or exclude in a Personal Profile is perhaps the great dilemma of internet dating. There is a fine line – and sometimes that line is thick and inaccurately drawn – between stating truths that might not be as alluring as possible or offering information that could be construed as being less than 100% factual in hopes of generating interest.

Exaggerations are not uncommon. Self-evaluation can, on occasion, be overly generous. When presenting ourselves to others, we prefer to accentuate the positive. Flaws are understandably held in abeyance. We all do it. It's expected.

But at some point, the omissions and exaggerations come home to roost.  As Desi was fond of telling Lucy, "you got some 'splainin'; to do."

Such was the case that evening.

The picture that Mona posted online was indeed a lovely shot and, to be fair, it was definitely a photograph of her.

But it was not current – or even relatively current. Quite possibly it was taken within a recent decade. But even that may be cutting it close.

Unfortunately, the intervening 20 or so years had not been kind to Mona. Even allowing for the wear and tear of her recent driving experience in the deluge, her visual appearance was somewhat less than a pleasant surprise. Her dour expression did nothing to enhance, nor did the additional pounds she had difficulty concealing.

To say the least, both of us knew right from the get-go that we were well on the way to a less than perfect evening.

Admittedly, Mona had done all of the hard work – driving for well over an hour in a downpour while I did nothing but wait in my apartment - dry, comfortable and totally relaxed. Her mood, quite understandably, was not good. Not good at all.

For me, the letdown was of another kind. In preparation for the evening, I had the loft cleaned, orderly and in great shape. As soon as I knew she was going to be delayed I had food delivered so she'd have something to eat immediately upon arrival. I set the table and had a sufficient supply of good wine ready to be poured. I was high on anticipation but the instant I opened the door and saw that she was not the person I had been expecting, my mood turned.

After a less than promising beginning, to the shock of neither of us, the rest of the evening continued to go downhill.

Mona was a bit taken aback by my apartment. For New York, it's quite large - two floors, each with 14-foot ceilings. There's a pretty slick chef's kitchen that, as an incompetent chef, I use only to make coffee or microwave whatever the delivery guy brings. I also have a pretty quirky collection of art that's hard to ignore. (Mine may be the only home with a few hundred cookie jars and a wall mounted-bowling alley). Most people like my place. For Mona, it was overwhelming. From the moment she entered she was intimidated and uncomfortable. Also, cold, aggravated and soaked.

To ease the tension and help mellow things out, I offered her a drink. It seemed a reasonable thing to do. But it turned out to be a failed attempt. What I had to offer was a poor match for what she desired. I had wine, beer, juice, sparkling water and a full liquor cabinet but, sadly, no mixers.

Mona was appalled. "No Coke?"

It's been several years since I've thought of Coke as a mixer but that was beside the point. I had none. Even worse, I had no other soft drinks, either.

Reluctantly, she agreed that wine would suffice. Here at least, I knew I was in good shape. I brought out a decent bottle of red and, while I was opening it, she had another request:

"Could I have lots of ice with that?"

She could. And she did. But that doesn't mean she liked it.

The discomfort was palpable. From the instant we were face to face, we both knew that nothing but doom and gloom lay ahead. And unfortunately, an immediate departure was out of the question. Mona was stuck because the journey home was a long one and the rain that continued to come down would only make it longer and more frustrating. She needed at least some time to calm down and prepare for the return trip home. So we had no choice other than to play out the bad hand that we had dealt ourselves. But no matter how quickly Mona would be able to leave, we both knew that this was going to be a long evening.

What happened during the time we spent together is a complete blur. I don't know what we talked about or how we managed to pretend to have polite conversation. The food that had been delivered didn't help much. Appetites tend to diminish when foul moods escalate. I'm sure we ate something. I doubt if either of us enjoyed anything.

Despite the awful weather, it was obvious that Mona couldn't wait to leave. As soon as she possibly could, she told me that she really had to be going. I didn't even pretend to offer a protest.

From the moment she announced her intended departure until the second the door shut behind her, not even a minute elapsed.

Wham. Bam. Goodbye ma'm.

Needless to say, this was hardly sad farewell. Although outside it was pouring cats and dogs, here inside, there was not a wet eye in the house.

All in all, there is no question that Mona got the worst of it. She spent long, frustrating, uncomfortable hours in her car in order to spend an even more uncomfortable hour or less with me.

I, on the other hand, never left the comfort of my home the entire evening. And, after she left, I still had an almost full bottle of wine.

Which I drank in its entirety.

Without ice.

# Sometimes you win.
# Sometimes you lose.
# And sometimes you're just an asshole.

I have been wrestling with myself about whether to include or exclude this section. It is yet to be determined whether the fact that it remains can be recorded as a victory or defeat.

As you will see if you choose to continue (a task that is neither recommended nor encouraged), this is one of the lengthier episodes even though it is not particularly amusing. It would have been easy to edit a significant portion of the exchanges without harming the spirit of the conversation but, for good or ill, they remain intact and reveal the arc of the story as it unfolded.

Spoiler alert:  there is no surprise conclusion. Elizabeth and I don't end up together. More warnings: no consequential truths are revealed and there is nary a chuckle to be found anywhere. How and why the relationship ramped up and ultimately ended may be of some interest, but even that is certainly open to question.

My justification for inclusion is that it's an important, albeit unhappy, reminder that the process of trying to find "the one" almost inevitably involves missteps along the way. Sometimes there are near misses, sometimes there are hilarious misses and sometimes there are abject failures.

Elizabeth, however, didn't fit comfortably into any of those categories.

For the most part, I was able to walk away from my failed attempts with limited guilt. Often the ending occurred sufficiently early. No harm, no foul. Equally often I believed that the woman and I shared a common belief that we were equally pleased about not being a couple. In all of those

243

cases, it wasn't difficult to escape with my emotions and integrity intact.

But the Elizabeth saga did not allow me to walk away with head held high. As is true with all too many "growth experiences", the lesson was not enjoyably learned.

Technically, Elizabeth and I never actually broke up because we were never really together. Even when early indications show that the stars seem to be in full alignment there is no assurance that one of them won't fall, shoot off into space or burn out prematurely.

Life is a bumpy road. The journey is not always pleasant. Sometimes the problem is due to a poorly paved boulevard but often fault for the rocky trip can only be blamed on driver error.

I don't offer the Elizabeth story with pride. I include it because it was part of my on-going search - a search that had a number of truly enjoyable highs, a significant number of amusing failures and some undeniable lows.

This, unquestionably, was the lowest.

The narrative begins with an email from Elizabeth.

*Hello, H........*

*Imagine. This is my fledgling email to a personal on my 3-day-old laptop.*

*Your profile "spoke to me" as they say....seems we have a great deal in common. Unfortunately, I don't have the photo and the profile and all of that hooked up, so I can only hope I can pique your interest with words at this point.*

*I'm 49, live in NYC, 5' 5", attractive, pretty fit, dark hair and brown eyes....like you, I got out of the advertising/agency rat race some years ago....but eased into the arts marketing/cultural world (happen to love my job).*

*Without a picture, you'll have to "picture" me for now. My best features are probably my smile, my brains, and my legs.....and with a great mixture of intelligence and humor, can only hope to make you "delirious" at some point (that was the part of your profile that made me smile!)*

*Do email me?*

*I look forward to it. Oh.....my name is Elizabeth*

Hi Elizabeth -

I'm honored to be the recipient of the maiden voyage of your Personal responses.

You may soon find that responding to Personals ads is an experience akin to looking for a new home. At first there is unbridled excitement and enthusiasm. That is followed, almost immediately by the disappointment of reality. The number of people who have nothing to say and little to offer is almost infinite. But, nevertheless, they're out there, flailing away, sucking up space, time and energy.

Of course, you and I are not amongst that group - something they all say, along with the inevitable, "I look much younger than my age".

Anyway, it was great to receive your reply and read your photo-description. I have always been a leg man and, as I explained in my profile, brains, to me, are any person's most attractive feature.

It was also interesting to learn that you actually have a job that you like. That, especially in these difficult times, is surely a rarity.

I'm certainly up for continuing the correspondence if you are. Would you rather proceed by email or phone? Either is fine with me.

Thanks for writing,

Howie

*Hello Howie –*

*How fortunate I am that the object of my "maiden voyage" through aol personals has not only responded, but actually holds my interest!*

*Thank you for the words of advice....already, I trust that you're on the mark.*

*In answer to your question...in short time, I'd probably prefer to talk on the phone. So much nicer to dialogue in "real time" but for now, hope to hear back from you via email while you work on establishing my "comfort level" (you're doing very well, for starters, should you care to know).*

*Have a good Sunday. I'll check messages tonight. I'll admit, I'm looking forward to knowing more about you.*

*You intrigue me.*

*Elizabeth*

**Note:**

There is a missing email from me. But it's pretty easy to deduce at least some of its content. With what was intended to be a modicum of wit, I seem to have explained that I worked for an advertising agency, lived downtown and proved that I had the ability to write at least a few grammatical sentences with only a minor number of spelling errors.

Whatever the precise content and style of the missing email might have been, it was sufficient to generate this response from Elizabeth.

*H –*

*Well.....you intrigue me more and more.*

*Imagine -- you manage to make me laugh when I'm all alone. And, the more you reveal, the more I like it!*

*I don't mean to be mysterious...it's a bit like peeling an onion. Let me try to tell you more.*

*This could take a while...hope you have time!*

*Like you, I worked in advertising (specifically direct marketing -- mostly agency side) all of my adult life. Managed to be CEO of a Ted Bates subsidiary when I was 32 (and with a five week old child at the time. Loved what I did....just did too much of it, in that I was heavily into that "superwoman" thing. And along with lots of travel (you had pharmaceuticals....I had Greek and Puerto Rican Tourism along with a number of cruise lines and a bevy of others/fashion, cosmetics and techs). Came back to the office from Venezuela one day and realized I'd missed the first year and a half of my son's life, and began implementing some changes...including leaving the agency to consult (very successfully) for a few years and have another child.*

*Upon becoming a single parent (11 years ago....wow, time goes by) with then 3 and 6 year old sons (yes...they're now 14 and 17) I got a little "closer to home" and made a move into arts marketing -- then, working in a museum that I could walk to work from was almost like semi-retirement (it kept me physically and emotionally available to my kids tho).....and, for the last 8 years, I've been marketing director of a major performing arts org. And yes, I do love what I do. Great atmosphere, great perks....and still fun.*

*And, in my "spare" time, I write for a number of magazines - usually on the subjects of antiques, decorating and collectibles.*

*Have raised my kids myself....and am just beginning to see the "light at the end of the tunnel" (my "vacation" later this month is driving across the entire state of Pennsylvania and back taking my older son on college tours/interviews).*

*I live in Brooklyn (Park Slope.....so after nearly 25 years here, I've watched it become gentrified and beyond...and, you can bet I am thankful that I bought my brownstone more than 18 years ago!) and work in the Lincoln Center area.*

*I'm very well traveled....a bit of the reverse of you....haven't done as much traveling in the states as I used to in year's past (and have been feeling the yen)....but have covered lots of ground in Europe, North Africa, S. America and the Caribbean....including 3 trips to Barbados this year between December and April (I have a helluva tan).*

*I like a good adventure and know how to enjoy myself. I know how to laugh, I'm optimistic (probably to a fault) and am passionate about what I do and who I love.*

*Life is full....but, I'll tell you -- I enjoy men, and like having one in my life....and at the moment, there is no one "special", having ended a relationship about 4 months ago.*

*It's late now, and I'm tired. Forgive me for being so long-winded....but you know how it is when you and I get talking!*

*OK......so, let's spin out the intrigue a little longer and peel a few more layers off the onions w/our email (I've enjoyed yours very much so far)....*

*Until I hear from you again,*

*Elizabeth*


Hi Elizabeth -

It's amazing that you find me intriguing. I'm not very much a man of mystery. Ask the people who've worked with me. They think I'm as subtle as a kick in the nuts. (But I do it very gently, so it feels more like a massage). Few people leave a meeting muttering, "I wonder what Howie REALLY thinks." Usually, I'm pretty clear. OK, painfully clear.

You, on the other hand, by saying much more, offered information leading to lots of additional questions. Some of which, I'll probably ask.

Question one: I understand about peeling onions, but have you ever sliced one? Frankly, that's what I usually do. I peel oranges. Onions, I slice and dice.

Now, on to the single parent part: where was your husband for the last 11 years? Were you a single parent and the sole source of income or were the kids living with you while your ex-husband at least participated in their lives to some degree?

My ex-wife and I have been apart for almost 20 years. For a while, she tried to take care of the boys (they were 6 and 8) after we split. After a year, it was obvious that she couldn't, so I took them. As far as a career move, it wasn't very good. But as far as a life move, it couldn't have been better. There was plenty of testosterone flying around our house with 3 males and no females. There was no one to say "don't do that in the house" or "if you don't finish your vegetables you won't get dessert" or "you're not going to wear THAT to school."

Essentially we had two rules: Until something breaks or someone cries, anything is acceptable. Not surprisingly, lots of things broke. Surprisingly, there were very few tears.

You've alluded to the "major performing arts organization" twice. Does it have a name? Does it have something to do with Barbados?

Antiques, decorating and collectibles - I think we have a match. Of course, there are all kinds of antiques, all kinds of decorating and all kinds of collectibles - but I'm into all 3. My own tastes are pretty varied, but I'm not very big on the European stuff (probably no real surprise there). At one time I had quite a bit of early American furniture. Got rid of it a long time ago. My decorating style has run the gamut: once it was just garbage: Danish modern, earth tones and all the crap that I thought was tasteful when I was young. Then I moved into my American period - lots of pine, some oak, some clocks. After the divorce, I went stark modern. I wouldn't allow any wood in the house. Now, in NY, I've simply gone goofy. I have lots of art - most of it quite unusual (for example, I have a bowling alley on the wall), some furniture that I designed (but someone else made), and my very important collection of cookie jars.

The "looking at colleges" trip is wonderful. I did it with both boys and had a ball. I went in the summer (looks like you're doing the same) which is not the best. When school isn't in session, it's difficult to get a true feel for the place. Still, you do get to see a lot - and it's amazing how all colleges are both similar and different at the same time. The most impressive thing, invariably, is when you take the first tour and the student guide talks to you while walking backwards. After that, it's all down hill.

What schools are you looking at? I've been getting closer and closer to buying land In Pennsylvania (about a half hour outside of Philadelphia, near the Delaware border). There are lots of reasons for doing that, but one of them is because there are so many good colleges nearby - and teaching at the college level has been in the back of my mind for a long time.

I know a little about Park Slope. About 4 years ago I was in a relationship with a woman who lived in a brownstone there. I don't think she bought as early as you did, but as soon as the word got around that Elizabeth had made the investment, the land rush was on. 4 years ago Park Slope was already very good - my guess is that it's gotten much better since then.

You may be one of the last living adults who boasts of a tan. I've always been impressed with the look, but after reading so much about skin cancer (one of our clients is Schering Plough, the maker of Coppertone) and spending time with my dermatologist, I'm pale and I'm proud.

My last relationship ended about 6 months ago - which, I guess, makes me 2 months readier than you. I really enjoy the together part when it's working, but the breaking up part truly sucks. It takes me a long time to pick myself off of the floor - even if I'm the one who called it off.

Another question: how do you combine the man in your life with the boys in your life? At what point do they get to know each other? And, assuming they got to know the men, how did the boys react when you split up? For me, the situation was impossible. I knew my responsibilities for raising the boys, trying to earn a living, and taking care of my ex-wife (she was both physically and emotionally ill) were all that I could handle. I really didn't date with an attitude towards having a serious relationship until the boys were about 14 and 16. Although they knew some of the women I was seeing casually, the boys also knew that they were my highest priority. I've often thought about the situation and wondered if I did the right thing. The message they received was: it's not important to have a relationship with a woman. After all, dad's doing fine and we're doing fine, so who needs women? Fortunately, they rejected that message: both of them are in relationships with women who are terrific in their own right, and even better as part of a couple.

Enough onion peeling?

OK. Now that you're back home from that mysterious job, it's time to feed the boys and get to work on that tan (although even an expert practitioner such as yourself may have some difficulty doing that after the sun goes down).

Mr. Intrigue,
Howie

**Note:**

The next email from Elizabeth was a tough one.

The subject line read "FASCINATION" but there was absolutely nothing in the email itself. Not a single word. There was no message at all. My interpretation was that she actually sent me a message and it was something on the order of: "You want to know what my fascination level is? It's zero. Too insignificant to even write anything at all."

Even though we were in the very early stages of writing to each other, I was surprisingly disturbed. But an hour later the real email came through.

*Hello, Howie*

*SO many questions......and me without a printer hook up for this computer and having to respond by memory.....let's see what I can do.*

*But first -- re: the onion and the intrigue. The onion, I realize, was probably stuck in my subconscious because of a book I read and left laying around the house, only to be mocked by my sons, called "Peel My Love Like an Onion" -- bad name, good book -- takes place within the flamenco circuit (I love flamenco, by the way....that is -- as you say -- observing more than participating! And, just found out that my little group that I follow is in NY for 3 weeks at the Public Theater -- Noche Flamenca -- they're great).....but I do like the image of the "onion peeling" as our story unfolds....it has the potential to be a tear jerker!*

*In terms of the "intrigue"....I meant that, actually, as less mysterious than fascinating. In fact, you're not mysterious at all, in the sense that you're "withholding" information....I just like what's unfolding....I'm finding it fascinating -- certainly intriguing -- that I could connect with someone like you, from out of the ozone....a complete stranger (and I suspect you are strange)....who can so hold my interest.*

*I think you're quite a guy, already.*

*Let's see - next question. I've been single for nearly 11 years. I'm divorced from a man who didn't want to leave, and as a result is one bitter guy who had trouble separating his issues with me from the kids.....so yes, I have been sole support and single parent to them and he has had little contact with them in all these years and no contact whatsoever for the last 6 years....although he lives right in the Village. I had a number of very tough years (I know what you mean about it not being the best career move!) but I don't really like to rake it over the coals, so I don't talk about it much (lucky for you). Lucky for my kids, they seem to be oddly well adjusted.*

*As for the men and the boys - interesting question. It was difficult, not ever having a night off or "alternate weekends" like other single parents.....and I was very respectful, always, of the role I was modeling for my kids in the sense that.....although, yes, I generally had....and have....a man in my life (serial monogamist?)....I was never casual about having a man sleep over, and was always home in my bed when they woke up in the morning.  Now that we're "all older" I'm "allowed to have sleepovers" if I'm "seriously involved with someone"....just not here.....and just if " they don't have  to think about it or picture it"*

*In terms of introducing men friends to my kids.....I'd rather not.....and, frankly have avoided getting involved with men who have children (now that I'm getting old, and the men are getting older too, I'm just plain lucky when someone has grown  children....they have the experience and can relate, without bringing their kids along!)*

*Given their situation with their absentee father, of course, I'd love to shield them from men coming in and out of their lives.....in theory.....I say that, because in truth, it hasn't worked that way.  So many times, I've assumed men will want to avoid having relationships with my kids but they form them anyway....and then get so caught up with my kids that they want to continue relationships with them, even after we end ours.  My kids used to jokingly tell me that "I'd have no boyfriends if it weren't for them".*

*OK....so now, we've established that I have charming and well adjusted children.*

*But seriously, I think I took a different approach than you did w/your kids.  My kids knew that I wasn't "turned off to men" after my divorce, or no matter my ups and downs with men....that, I hope, I had a healthy attitude about* relationships....and we'd often entertain ourselves on Sunday mornings playing a favorite family game of ours -- "Rate the Date". Don't even get them going on the topic of my "bad boyfriends"!

This IS a long email.....what's with us? Can you imagine when we get phones in our hands!

I love your letters by the way.....they're very engaging. And speaking of the many things that I find engaging about you....I was playing Etta James (At Last) when I came upon your Personal (wow, man!) and discovered Nina Simone when I was 12.

What else, what else? The tan....yes, I know, I must be crazy. Spent a lot of time on the beach this winter and just couldn't stop. I'm seeing a dermatologist next week, and he'll probably tan me alive! (But hell, it looks good!)

Barbados? Where, obviously, I was spending a lot of time on the beach. No....that wasn't work, it was my last relationship, actually. Went down there to be alone for a few days - to "get away from it all" (I've long known that nothing gives me peace and relaxes me like being on or near the sea and had a "romantic encounter" with a white native Bajan (there are probably 12) and frankly, got caught up in the fantasy. We were alternating his coming here and my going there....but the cultural void was just too huge to bridge. His family went back to the 1600's there....sugar....and he was more than bigoted, he was a colonialist! I'm just a liberal, NY Jew....what can I say....it became "intergalactic"......but, believe me, that was a tough one to give up on, given my rich fantasy life.

So many more questions.....but, this is getting too long. Guess we'll have to "talk" some more?

I'm going to end it for now and nurse the burn on my finger from the marvelous dinner I cooked tonight (I put so much

255

*of myself into my cooking!) I'm an ok cook (tho it's not a passion of mine), but must say, I'm a great baker!*

*I look forward with eager anticipation to your next installment.*

*goodnight for now,*

*Elizabeth*


Hi Elizabeth –

Brace yourself. This will be a long, but hopefully, good one. It may fall into the TMI (too much information) category, but you get to be the judge of that.

I'm going to take a small turn to the left (I believe for both of us that would be the politically correct direction), take a chance, and write from a somewhat different point of view. I'll still try to keep things relatively humorous when possible. But because there is so much in our email exchange that I find fascinating, exciting, and enormously encouraging, I also feel the need to explain what happened last night.

Ever since my Personal Profile went online a little over a week ago, I've suddenly become Mr. Popular. I've received at least 50 replies and responded to many of them. That has resulted in some spirited, engaging and positive back and forth emails. But, to be honest, there has been little emotion in it for me. Out of the entire first wave of respondents there had been only one person I was even interested in meeting - and that is a long, relatively astonishing story which will have to wait for a later time (it is, however, well worth waiting for). With all the others, I was simply going through the motions.

I can't pinpoint what made me perk up so quickly to your response, but suffice it to say that I felt an immediate sense of heightened interest. From then on, I looked forward to your emails with greater anticipation than I held for any others.

Yesterday – last night to be precise – I received an email from you that stopped me cold. Before I go on, let me assure you that the end of this story comes out extremely well. But, for about an hour, I was a very unhappy boy. Here's what happened. I checked my in-box and there was a message from you. The subject was "Fascination". I opened the message and it was completely blank. Nothing. Zero. Not a word.

I quickly did a check to see if something had gone awry. Perhaps you'd sent a message and the words got erased. Perhaps you'd sent it inadvertently. Perhaps I'd opened it incorrectly. Although I had no idea what I was looking for – or even what I'd do if I found it - nevertheless I pressed on.

But then I realized that the message was absolutely clear. You'd meant to send no words. In fact, saying nothing was infinitely more powerful than saying a lot. For you, there no longer was any "fascination." It simply didn't exist. You'd completely written me off.

The first thing that happened at that moment of realization was that all the air went out. Then my mind started to race: what had I said that could turn you off so completely?

So I re-read my last email to you. And I viewed it from a completely different perspective. I wanted to find out how my best intentions had resulted in such a negative interpretation. From that vantage point, I saw problems everywhere. I felt simply awful.

My first inclination was to send you an email that contained only two words: "brilliantly phrased."

257

I wanted to let you know that I understood the statement (the non-statement) you had made.

Then I thought...that's not enough. Because if I only sent those two words, there would be no chance to move forward. I would simply have accepted your powerful statement of non-interest.

At this point I was feeling terrible. Somehow, despite my best intentions, I had ruined something that felt very important to me. I didn't want to walk away. I didn't want to say, "if that's the way she feels, the hell with her." I wanted to find some way to correct the situation.

So I tried to think of something.

First I was going to offer a short, terse apology. That didn't seem sufficient. But, what else could I do? At one point I even considered sending you an annotated version of my previous email. I'd explain what I meant by every paragraph, where I'd said too much, not said enough, failed in attempts at humor, etc. All in the way of offering profuse apologies.

But instead of doing anything, I took a break. A friend was over at my apartment (long story – explained some other time) and we just watched TV for an hour. Frankly, I didn't pay much attention to the tube. I just looked at it while my mind raced in an attempt to figure out how to solve a situation that I had so completely botched.

At the end of the TV show, I came downstairs, checked my email and found a long, spectacular, charming, fascinating email from you.

It's difficult – even for me – to explain how my mood changed. I can only compare the situation to finding a lost wallet. You know how you feel when you first realize that the wallet is missing? There's no one to blame, there's a lot of personal stuff lost, there's a feeling of emptiness, and a sense of frustration. Every minute the search goes on, the desperation mounts. The pit in the stomach gets deeper. You just feel rotten.

Then, magically, somehow, the wallet appears. At that moment, the relief is almost overwhelming. All is right with the world. You can actually feel breath return to your body.

The more I read you email, the better I felt. There is, as I said before, something very strange happening. Writing via the computer is fairly impersonal. Yet I "feel" who you are. It's not so much reading between the lines – it's simply understanding the words at a depth that goes beyond the sentences.

When I placed my profile in the Personals, I limited my desires to brains and humor. While they are of enormous importance to me, they are, by no means, all that I require. As I've gotten older, I've gotten more demanding. In order for me to make a true connection, I crave so much more. But, if I had listed all of my hopes in the ad, my fear is that no one would have responded.

Yet here are some of the things that I've observed about you – things that are monumentally attractive to me.

A sense of the positive. I've been with people who discuss whether the glass is half full or half empty. My take is that for most of them – regardless of what they say - the glass is bone dry. They take pleasure in complaining - in fact that is often their only means of communicating. I see none of that in you. Everything you said was positive – the way you feel about your job, your experiences and, most of all, your boys. Even your description of men who are no longer a significant part of your life treats them kindly.

Communication with children. Parenting, I believe, is the single most difficult job...ever. There is no way to get it right enough. There is no way to say "I did all that I could." But, there is a way to derive pleasure for your children. To interact with them. To tell them that what they say to you is important. To let them know that they can make you laugh – even if you are the object of the laughter. You get that. I know so many people who don't even understand that such a thing is even possible.

It's useless to wallow in self-pity. So many people feel the world has dealt them unfair blows and that is their excuse for failure. You, on the other hand, looked reality in the eye, determined what you had to do, and then got it done. I have always been incredibly attracted to strong women, and your strength is visible everywhere.

Sometimes you just have to give it a shot. Like it or not, reality surrounds us. The reasons NOT to do something, NOT to even try are manifold. But sometimes, even in the face of great odds, there is enough good to be gained from merely stepping into the water that it makes the prospect of becoming completely soaked well worth the effort. Your episode with the Sugar Baron made me smile. I hope you enjoyed every minute of the implausible ride.

Now, a valuable lesson. If you get nothing else out of this exchange, you are soon to be rewarded with something worthwhile. You complained that you didn't have a printer, so it was hard to keep track of all my questions. Well...here's the solution.

After you read an email that you want to respond to, just highlight the whole thing and copy it. Then, after you hit the "reply" button push the "paste" button and the entire email will appear. You can refer to it as you write your response – and then, simply erase any portion as you go. You don't need a printer because the email will be right in front of you the whole time.

On to more important topics: flamenco. I know nothing about it – although I can certainly recognize when it is being danced. If you're up for seeing Noche Flamenca, let's do it. You can astound me with your vast knowledge or just fake it – I'll be a willing and gullible audience.

Still can't quite get behind the onion peeling concept. Peeling something away, layer by layer, is a good idea if the core is truly special. With onions, after the dry outer skin is gone, it's all good. I know the phrase, I just never really thought about it before. And if I find someone I can complain to, I'm gonna let them know.

I'm right with you in terms of the way you deal with the men in your life and how they interact with your sons. It's a very delicate subject. I understand how men can find smart, happy boys to be an attraction. Bonds are easily formed – especially when the boys don't have a father as a role model. Sounds to me like you kept the focus pretty clear – especially the way you and your sons discussed the situation. And, by the way, the boys do sound quite wonderful – as does the way that you talk about and with them.

I wasn't so much "turned off" by women after my divorce, as I was unable to focus on them. I may have sounded flippant when I said my wife was both physically and emotionally ill. Unfortunately, that's the truth. She had a variety of addictions: she was an anorexic, a bulimic, a smoker and a drinker. And, as if that wasn't enough, she also spent sustained periods in mental institutions. She just called me today – after being released from yet another one. It's a very sad story because she is truly a kind and generous person. She is simply unable to cope with the world.

That Etta James was singing when you read my Profile is a little too ooga booga for me. Even though I was very much a child of the 60's, I never was a big believer in cosmic moments. Still...

Sorry you burned yourself cooking. I've been doing so much with raw fruits and vegetables that I seldom even use my stove. I have a giant, restaurant stove that I use, essentially, to boil water for tea. It's an art form, and one I have come pretty close to mastering.

At this moment, I have no idea how to press on with you. The emails are delicious. No doubt talking would be equally wonderful. The real question is: will we meet while you still sport that glorious tan? There are some things in life that simply should not be wasted.

Howie


*No subject.....read between the lines now. I'm speechless!*

*You fool! I was about to begin writing to you....explaining the fascination you held for me -- which seems inexplicable to me -- the subject was "fascination".*

*I inadvertently hit the enter button.*

*And....went right on to write you the long email.*

*You've left me in tears....and quite incapable of typing.*

*Call me asap at 718-000-0000.*

*I have to hear your voice soon.*

**Note:**

After this reply, I called her and set up a plan to get together on Saturday. I followed the phone call with this email:

Miss Elizabeth -

Yes, I know it's hot. Yes, I know it's been a rough day. Yes, I know this is a most difficult time at work.

But give it a rest honey - I can't put up with this constant bitching.

Do you hear me complaining? Even though the radio awakened me with a song that was not to my liking? Even though the NY Times was placed askew on my doormat? Even though there were not nearly enough raisins in my cereal? Did I mention it? Did I weigh you down with that information?

I think I've made my point.

On to more important material. Since you brought it up on our last phone conversation, I thought I'd elaborate. Yes, I do wonder what you look like. Here's what I expect:

Frankly, I've not been completely honest with you. All the stuff about brains and humor are really of no consequence to me. Essentially, I'm looking for a trophy. So, in addition to the great tan and great legs, I'm envisioning a wonderfully taught, shapely, but not overly muscled body. Slim waist, medium hips, small firm breasts (bras are laughably unnecessary) shoulder length auburn hair, and a face that never needs make-up yet still looks natural and wholesomely beautiful. I'm envisioning any of the women on "Friends" except much more attractive, of course.

263

I certainly hope I won't be disappointed.

And just think of what you'll be getting in return: a bald, bearded, four-eyed, Jew. Isn't that what every gorgeous woman wants?

No? You're kidding. You think they'd actually PREFER Brad Pitt? I'm shocked. Shocked and disillusioned.

I think I'm going to have to lie down (lay down?). Don't talk to me about grammar now - I'm too upset. Brad Pitt indeed. I'll call you tonight. And don't mention you know who.

Howie


**Note:**

This email followed another one that also contained no message. The subject line was "Brad Pitt my ass."


*H –*

*I do that sending w/o writing thing every time! Didn't mean it that time. What I was going to say was:*

> *"Brad Pitt, my ass...*

*...I've had the advantage of seeing a picture of YOU...and for my money you're much sexier."*

*It's working for me.*

*I'm in for the night...catch you later?*

**Note:**

What follows is the second email that Elizabeth sent. The first one was titled "never stop emailing me" but again it arrived completely blank. This time, however, I didn't panic. I knew the drill. And, as she explained in the beginning of her this message, the other one was sent inadvertently.

*DEAR Howie (note the emphasis)   -- I just did it again! I just figured out that if I double backspace, for some reason, which I just did.....and probably did the other night.....it sends the email before I get out of the "subject"*

*PLEASE don't be trying to figure out what I really meant! (Altho, it works for me as a profound message.....read between the lines if you will.)*

*How is it that you....whoever you are....have the ability to make me laugh out loud or cry (not too loud) just with your written word?*

*I've noticed that finding your email each night has become the best moment of my day...my reward. I'd love them to never stop.*

*Call me if you are home and get this....I'm good till about 11:00.*

*Just wanted to "reach out and touch you" before I left for work.*
*(I like having you be the last person I talk with before I fall asleep at night, you know....makes me feel all dreamy about you in the morning, I've noticed). I wake up thinking about you.*

*So here's what I woke up thinking about this morning....something wasn't sitting quite right with me about the plans we were making for tomorrow night. Even though this (certainly, in my opinion) isn't a typical first date, a typical blind date, a typical "Personals thing"....there doesn't seem to be anything "typical" about anything that's happened between us for this last week...convention would dictate that I probably shouldn't be meeting you at your apartment for our first meeting. (And you know how conventional we are).*

*Why don't you choose a restaurant....or something along those lines...and let's meet there. We can always go back and hang out at your place afterwards, once we've established that you're not in fact a stalker, as rumor has it.*

*I need to establish that comfort level -- right? I feel certain that that should take us all of about a minute or so.*

*You ok with that? Hope tomorrow comes soon.*

*E*


Miss Elizabeth –

Well... what a wonderful way to start the day. I expected only business info on my computer but what I got instead was another in a series of encouraging notes from you.

No problem about meeting someplace else. Although it is a bit difficult carrying the manacles, whips and handcuffs with me. I guess we'll just have to go to a restaurant where they're used to this kind of thing. Are you familiar with the Sado Masochistic Sushi Bar and Domination Hut? I've heard they do some amazing things with raw tuna.

Just so you know - the reason I suggested meeting at my place wasn't only to tie you up at knifepoint. My hope was that we could get together earlier, rather than having to wait until dinnertime to meet. Knowing how important hipness is to me, you can surely imagine my deep sense of embarrassment if we show up at a truly trendy restaurant in time to cash in on the early bird special.

But, of course, you're right (I hate that. I wanna be right too. Sometimes). When we speak tonight, we'll figure out the soonest you can reasonably get here. Then, because hopefully it won't be late enough for dinner, I'll have some thoughts about where we can meet in a totally public place where there will be absolutely no touching. And I mean that. Don't you even think about grabbing anything or one of the nearby downtown yentas will immediately come to my aid.

I just got back from the Frank Gehry exhibit. It was spectacular. This guy has completely redefined architecture. The show was incredibly energizing - lots and lots of models provided insight to his thought process. What's most amazing to me is that in addition to his free-form thinking and design, he's actually been able to convince people to pay for and build his structures. The Guggenheim that's planned for New York may well be his best ever. I can't wait.

OK. I've had it with your complaints about the heat, the rain, the traffic, the job. Fortunately, my life is still absolutely perfect. And I have every expectation that it's gonna get even better tomorrow.

Howie


**Note:**

Even though I was the one who wrote the last email, apparently I decided to start the day off with another one:

Good morning Miss Elizabeth -

For some reason, I didn't get a whole lot of sleep last night. I wonder why.

I've been trying to figure out what to wear today. My blue jeans? My blue, blue jeans? Or perhaps my jeans that are blue. How faded? How new? I'm sure you can imagine my dilemma.

The weather gods seem to be doing us some favors - with the exception of denying you sufficient morning rays for sun worshipping.

As they say, we'll talk. And then...

Howie


**Note:**

The subject line for the next email from Elizabeth was "you make me feel like Meg Ryan."

It arrived the morning after we met at a restaurant and spent the day together. What transpired that day is easily determined by the information in the emails that follow.

*Howie –*

*I really like my new routine of coming home (early, you'll notice), turning on my computer and hearing that lilting Tom Hanks-ish "You've got mail!".*

*You'd better be all you seem cracked up to be....because I am in LOVE Howie, BABY!*

*Well, here it is 5:56 in the a.m......one would think I'd be sleeping the sleep of the dead, but instead I'm tossing and turning, so it's go to the beach or talk to you. You win, because it's dark out there.*

*What could be on my mind, keeping me up when I should be sound asleep with a smile on my face?*

*Worse than your own dilemma of yesterday, regarding how blue should be the blue jeans you chose, is my own of this morning... can I possibly respect a man such as this...a **slut**, who allows me to have my way with him on this, our 8th date?*

*Should AOL be advised of his unseemly behavior?*

*Is he that wanton....that depraved....that he allows himself to be lured back to his torrid love nest in the heart of Tribeca, that teaming fleshpot...by every predatory woman who responds to his AOL personal?*

*Who is the stalker here...and who the stalk-ee?*

*Have I frightened him...this young innocent...or have I dragged him down with me to the depths of depravity, where he will now wallow in sin and lust, forever more...wanting, craving, demanding MORE and MORE and MORE....*

*Oh God...I do hope so.*

*Our first/eighth date, for me, was in keeping with everything else I've experienced with you in this long and lucky week. It was sublime.*

*Elizabeth*

Miss Elizabeth -

GO TO SLEEP!

Was it still dark at 6 a.m. in Brooklyn? It's shiny and bright in sunny Manhattan at that time of the morning - except today when it was rainy and dark.

I did sleep - the sleep of the incorrigible, the naughty, and the well satisfied.

For only our 8th date, we certainly did good. Frankly though, i have no idea what you were referring to about debauchery. My feeling is that as long as my eyes are closed, I have no responsibility (or memory) of what occurs. So, by that logic, both of us are still as pure and virginal as we were at the beginning of the evening. Which means, if we're to examine the depths of sexual pleasures, we'll have to save that for a future occasion. My guess is that we'll be able to find the time.

Jesse called today - he's having young adult problems. All that's troubling to him now are his love life and his financial life. And, unfortunately, there are no easy answers for either. We're going to spend some time together this evening, but I don't know if there's much I can do that will truly help. I can certainly offer advice regarding money, but the other issue is much more complex and also much more important.

Get some sleep tonight. Hopefully you'll be exhausted enough to go to bed early. Remember, tomorrow is a school day. Well it is, if you work at a music hall - as opposed to, say, ...nowhere. By the time you've been up and at 'em for 3 hours, I'll still be considering whether to hit the Snooze bar one more time. For me, that's about as close to physical labor as I'm likely to get.

Howie

*Hello, Howie....well I did go to sleep -- took a nice long nap from about 9:00 until noon....these days are just full of unusual occurrences for me.*

*Don't worry about the time if you feel inclined to call tonight...I'd love to hear from you.*

*Elizabeth*


Hi girl -

Just got back from dinner with Jesse.

Even though you said it was OK to call, it felt too late to me. A working girl needs her beauty sleep.

So get some sleep, wake up early and tote that music. Make us proud.

I'll catch up with you tomorrow.

Howie


**Note:**

We didn't talk that night which probably meant that a phone call from me was in order the next day. But I didn't call. Instead, I wrote...

Hi Elizabeth -

Well, how does it feel to be back at Carnegie Hall even without years of practice. (Sorry, I know it's an old joke). A bit of advice: you guys could do well to take a few tips from the folks at the Grand Ole Opry. They put on one helluva show. People come from all over to listen, laugh, hoot and clap along. How many times does your audience break into spontaneous white people rhythmic clapping? Something to keep in mind.

I'm still very much into not sleeping. I'm sure there is a benefit hidden in there somewhere, but at the moment, it's a complete mystery to me. I've caught up on a lot of very bad mid to early morning TV, started and stopped some novels that couldn't hold my attention, and set a new record for tosses and turns.

Jesse is still stressed out - and for a lot of very good reasons. His girlfriend may be moving to Los Angeles, he's not sure if he will have to quit his job in order to tour with a band he really likes, and some of the stuff he left in the old apartment seems to have been thrown away as it was being readied for sale. He doesn't handle stress very well, and he's now feeling stressed about absolutely everything. By the time I left him last night he seemed to be doing fine - but based on today's phone call, he's gone right back to the bad place.

I got my 3 hours of phone conversations taken care of today. Almost all of it with one guy. But, I also snuck in a lunch with a long-time friend. I met him when he was still in college, and now his oldest daughter is nearly college age. It's amazing how all of these people have aged while I continue to be 30. It's easy to do - I just avoid mirrors and truth tellers.

That's it from downtown. What's the scoop in Brooklyn?
Howie

*Dear Howie --*

*I'm probably breaking every "rule" in the book by writing this email to you (I actually had a friend who I confided in about our experience today tell me I should play "hard to get" and not respond to an email or phone call from you for 72 hours....but I cannot even imagine playing games with you. It's not my style to begin with....but, certainly not with you).*

*So, here's the thing. You know that pivotal email you sent me last Tuesday night, where you were so unusually reflective, sensitive and forthcoming about your feelings...the one where you told me how it made you feel when you assumed I was writing you off....the one that made me simply fall in love with you before we'd ever even met? Well, because you had the courage to send me that email, I'll respond in kind and share with you all I'm feeling right now as I go through a similar experience.*

*This has been a very moving and happy period of time for me....since we began our correspondence.*

*I've never connected with a "stranger" in such a way. I've never just met someone who I so enjoyed, admired, respected and felt I had so much in common with. It has been a joy and a pleasure sharing our long and heartfelt emails and having our long bedtime talks.*

*Throughout it all, there was never a moment of awkwardness .... particularly when we met....which was a thrill and a relief to me.*

*But, now, since Sunday morning, I've been feeling nothing BUT awkwardness, and I wasn't expecting that.*

*First, let me tell you that I can't remember the last time I had sex on a first date....the early '70's maybe? I don't have "casual" sex.....but, for me, there has never been anything casual about what was going on between us. When I expressed my hesitance when we were at your apartment Sat. night and you told me that we should consider this our "eighth date", I decided to just let you guide me through it....to take that as an indication that you weren't feeling casual about this either...that there was something strange and special going on.*

*But, I'm a woman, after all....and a bit of a romantic.*

*I suppose I was expecting.....after the level of communication we had been having up until that night....and, yes, the romantic aspect it all seemed to hold....a "sign" from you that our "first/eighth" date, our meeting and yes, our making love, had meant something to you too.*

*An oom-pah band on my doorstep, perhaps...skywriting...flowers at the office this morning....but, certainly a phone call or a tender or encouraging email....a suggestion for when we'd meet again.*

*I told myself not to read too much into it yesterday when there was no call and then, finally, an email that did not have the usual "feeling"....but with each email to follow, they seem to be becoming more and more impersonal....until tonight's, which seemed to be the kind of detached and chatty note you'd send to a pal --- bringing me to read something into them (much like you experienced last Tuesday night with "fascination") which may or may not be there.*

*I could take this opportunity to fashion an email after your own of last Tuesday night....I could tell you how I feel a cold and constricting feeling inside my chest. I could share how now I am going over all I said and did on Saturday night that might have turned you off...or blown it. I could make a list for you of all the qualities I find monumentally attractive in you....share that I was beginning to feel like this was the "big one"....that all the others that had led up to you were merely place holders until I got to the real thing.....but, that would be going against those "rules" again....and, boy would I be embarrassed!*

*And, I'm not that stupid, am I?  How could I take such a risk....clearly, I'm not the man you are.*

*You are probably, among other things, the most honest and honorable man I'm ever likely to meet....so, I know you'll respond honestly, and not feel like I've put you on the spot.*

*If the chemistry just isn't there for you....if I wasn't what you'd expected, after all if you've decided to bring a bride over from Russia, I know that you could tell me plainly and kindly....tho, if that were the case, I'm not at all sure why the evening went on as long as it did or took the course it did on Saturday.  But, I'm a gunslinger...I can take it on the chin.*

*It's just that I recall last Tuesday, feeling a real and deep sense of remorse for causing you even one minute of doubt or sadness....and such awe and respect for you, that you were a man who could take a chance and tell me, without worrying that I would think you were desperate or "lame" that you cared.....and how it felt when you thought you'd blown it....lost me. I was moved, as you know, and touched.*

*So, for that reason, I'm writing all of this to you....which is an enormous risk, and what any woman I know would advise me is a big mistake.*

*For lack of anything more original to say, let me use your own very wise words...."at this moment, I have no idea how to press on with you...the real question is, will we meet (again) while I still sport that glorious tan? There are some things in life that simply should not be wasted."*

*So, now....for the first time, I feel very awkward.*

*Let me know what's on your mind, cause I can't take any more emails about the Grand 'Ol Oprey....tho I've been there and it's a fun night out for all.*
*Noche Flamenca this week....or do we become amusing email sending friends?*

*Elizabeth*


Dear Elizabeth -

Where to begin?  What to say?

First of all, there are no rules for you to break. This never was a game. It can't ever become one.

Everything you said makes perfect sense. It's true and it's from the heart. Now, let's see if I can reciprocate.

Saturday night was wonderful for me, too. It's kind of a hard thing to fake. You were everything I expected you'd be...and more. The brains and humor I already knew about. The passion was unanticipated, but incredibly welcomed. Everything about the night felt right.

I expected to sleep well. After all, I was exhausted and fulfilled. But sleep came only fitfully, and I woke Sunday morning in a cold sweat. And my stomach has been doing flip flops ever since.

Something is not right here - and the problem has nothing to do with you. I raced into this going full speed ahead with the best of intentions and the clearest of minds. And then, something inside me, pulled back. Is it fear of commitment? Possibly. Is it that if something is so good, I need to take it apart, examine it, and in the process, make it go away? No idea.

What I do know is that I have been anxiety ridden since Sunday morning. After we've been so close - and in many ways we were truly close long before we were intimate on Saturday night - suddenly I feel totally disconnected.

Was it something that you did or said? Absolutely not. OK, then why do I feel this way? I wish I had an answer.

There is a theory that we can control what we do, but not what we think, and not what we feel. I'd like to believe differently. I like to feel the way I felt all of last week - full of excitement and enthusiasm and anticipation and hope. But instead, I feel anxious, and uncomfortable, and awkward.

I don't know what to say. I don't know what to do. I've been incapable of calling - I guess that's obvious.

So...what now? I wish I knew. I don't think we're destined to be cute pen pals. But what will we be instead? I haven't a clue.

You're right - there should have been brass bands and skywriting and flowers. But I haven't been able to summon the emotional strength to even pick up the phone. I feel terrible. I have no words.

Howie

*Howie –*

*Well, I'm sorry that you wouldn't pick up the phone for my call....I'm not trying to chase you, you know, or make you uncomfortable....and I promise that I won't call or write again.*

*It just seems such a shame....I'd like to suggest that it's a stomach flu....but for the fact that I'm going through exactly the same thing.*

*You know I woke up at 5:00 am on Sunday morning after tossing and turning all night....and the feelings you describe, I share exactly.*

*But, maybe I'm just braver than you. Or, after a lifetime of Mr. Wrongs, can recognize a special connection when I see it.*

*But, alas....I'll wish you well and go have a good cry for myself.*
*If you have a change of heart -- just send those flowers.*

*You never did ask my last name. It's _____and you can send them in care of the XXXXX. I'll take that as a "sign" in lieu of skywriting.*
*All the best, always.....and no matter what -- I still think you're hot shit.*

*Love, Elizabeth*

**Note:**

That email was followed by another one. The subject line: "I've been thinking..."

It was the email that I dreaded.


*Howie –*

*...now, that my film persona has gone from the female lead of "You've Got Mail" to "Seduced and Abandoned"....and, I need to put it out there to you....to clear my head.*

*You knew that I was very new to "online dating"....so, I've been trying to piece this together since we talked on Monday night....if for nothing else, so I don't make this mistake again. And, of course, it would be a boon to womankind if you didn't make this mistake again either.*

*The way I figure it, one of a number of scenarios took place here:*

*-you were never sincere....and there's an old-fashioned, almost Victorian word for the way you behaved then, and that's a "cad".*

*-you were sincere at first, during the week of emailing and calling and was disappointed with the reality/there was no physical attraction for you....and in spite of knowing you'd be backing out the next morning, led me to have sex with you (even tho I was a willing participant, I don't recall initiating it, and know that you were aware that I was uncomfortable meeting at your apartment for our first face-to-face). So, if that was the case, to put it mildly....you behaved like an opportunist.*

*-But let me save face here. And, let's assume that you were sincere. That as you say, you weren't "faking" it. Let's just say you got "cold feet" the next morning. And, fell back on that Seinfeldian "it's not you, it's me".*

*As you say....the excitement, hopefulness, exhilaration of the email week just wasn't there when you woke up on Sunday.*

*Then, I'd say you behaved like a fool.*

*Flesh and blood reality cannot possibly be as exciting or mysterious as our fantasies.*

*It felt different for me too. But, Jesus....let's be adult about this.*

*Do you think it's appropriate to make a strong connection with someone, become close with them (albeit in a very brief period), share yourself with them, become intimate with them....and simply discard them the next day?*

*Do you think it's logical to find value in someone....let's assume you were sincere in what you told me. Here's a woman who you find to be intelligent, humorous, passionate....and she laughs at your jokes. Even if you were physically repulsed by me (which would bring me back to my "cad" theory....sorry)...do you de-value someone to the extent that you discard them because the reality wasn't as good as your fantasy? Do you mean that you could find no value in me at all on Monday morning...could not consider my feelings at all?*

*Emailing, I'm discovering, is a potent tool. You can pour your heart out, be creative, build a fantasy. Conjure up a romantic image that can't possibly stand up to cold reality.*

*All through Sat. night I felt a little bit detached. I was adjusting to the reality....it was different from my fantasy, you know.*

*Physically, you are not my "ideal", my "fantasy man", not even really my "type". I was aware of that immediately. You were a combination of many things, great and not so great....like any other real life human. My email fantasy was "better".*

*But yet....life's a compromise.....and I'm not 20, or even 30 any more. There were many things of value about you....there was a meaningful connection (or so I thought)....there were aspects that I could find attractive about you....and I wasn't merely looking to fall in lust. I was aware that there was a cerebral and emotional connection here, and that whatever we were to become....even if you weren't to be the "love of my life", surely you were a living, breathing, real person after all....and I put some value on you and on your feelings.*

*Surely, there was some place of value in my life for you....and weren't meant to be thrown out with the garbage the next day.*

*It's hard to adjust from the heady, hopeful images we conjure up with a faceless email romance.*

*But, real life isn't a Disney movie....it's real life. The earth rarely moves and lovebirds rarely twitter over our heads as in Snow White, when two people meet for real.*

*I thought -- hey, you're a smart guy, and you're not a kid, after all -- that after a couple of days you'd get this, and I'd hear from you.*

*Cold feet, I could forgive. Confusion, I could understand. Adjusting from the intoxication of online-romance fantasy to real life flesh and blood relating takes some reflection and understanding.*

*I get that.*

*I'm disappointed, disillusioned and hurt. I won't lie to you about that.*

*If you're not an opportunist and a creep (and, I don't in my heart, really think you are)....then you're at the least, perhaps, too self-reflective, overly analytical, painfully immature and far from grounded in reality.*
*You've behaved badly.*

*I don't know what either one of us has learned from this. I hope I've learned not to be so trusting, romantic or gullible.*

*You've disappointed me and hurt me deeply....more deeply than I would have thought possible in such a brief period of time.*

*The cyber version was very powerful....it moved at cyber speed. In real life, things go slower...but, if allowed to develop have much more going for them than mere fantasy. It will probably take me much more time to get over this than it took me to get into it.*

*E.*

**Note:**

A few hours later, this email arrived. The subject line: "Too much drama."

*Howie –*

*If I could take back that email I sent you this morning, I would. I'm embarrassed by it.*

*It was the unfortunate result of too many sleepless nights and too much re-hashing.*
*Well, we've seen the best and the worst sides of each other now....the darkest of my "dark side"....my issues with rejection and disappointment.*

*Quite simply, there's just been too much drama. From the start. Anything that builds to that height so quickly can only result in a big crash...it's not possible to sustain.*

*We both got caught up in the rush....it was too seductive. If it were possible to do it all over again, I for one, would do it much differently this time...but, I hope, if nothing else, I've learned something from my mistakes.*

*I was dealing with my own demons these past few days and when I sent that email, still groggy this morning, I thought it was my way of freeing myself of them....closing the door I'd left open so that I could avoid more disappointment.*

*Please forgive me...it was uncalled for.*

*Elizabeth*

**Note:**

That's it. That's all.

Of course Elizabeth was absolutely correct about everything – other than the need for me to accept her apology. She had nothing to apologize for. Today, almost two decades later, I still feel badly. And correctly so. What I did and what I didn't do were equally inappropriate.

What I did was what a lot of men do – let physical desire over-ride better judgment. I knew on the afternoon that we spent together that we were not destined to be a lifelong couple. The chemistry that had seemed so effortless in cyberspace did not find it's equal in real life. Physical attraction was no match for the magnetism that existed online or on the phone. Elizabeth indicated as much in one of her later emails. My feelings were similar. Let's leave at this: neither of us was visually intoxicated.

So how is it that we ended up having sex when both of us knew it was too soon and neither of us was overwhelmed with desire? Good question. I have no good answer. I don't even have a mediocre one,

Somehow, although definitely not in a fit of unbridled passion, we made the decision to cross the bridge that was definitely a bridge too far. I was hardly a reluctant participant but I definitely knew then what I continued to know from that moment on; it was a mistake. Even worse, it was a mistake that could never be corrected.

What I didn't do was write or call her again. I felt that there was nothing left to communicate and any attempt to explain or apologize would only prolong a situation that had nowhere to go but even further down.

Like almost everyone else, I have been in relationships that ended badly, emotionally or painfully. None occurred as hastily as this one. The accelerated timing in this case did not make for early healing; the speed with which it was accomplished was an active participant in causing pain.

Because the arc of what we created ascended so quickly my hope is that Elizabeth's recovery from my bad behavior was equally swift.

She is, as must be obvious, a wonderful person and surely deserved better. Because of who she is, I take some comfort in believing the chances are excellent that she has found it.

But that doesn't excuse my actions. And the fact that I am still troubled by what I did seems deservedly appropriate.

If there is a lesson to be learned here, it's hardly a surprising one. Poor judgment and bad behavior, while often avoidable, are also a part of life. We all make mistakes. Some can be corrected. Some cannot.

It would be an understatement to say that I'm not proud of my behavior. But it would have been foolish to believe that at least sometime during my online dating experiences, I would not do something regrettably inappropriate.

That is not intended as an excuse. Unquestionably I fully deserve all of the "shame on you's" tossed my way. It's further indication that hurt feelings can happen in cyberspace just as easily - and be just as devastating - as they can happen anywhere else.

On balance, my experiences in the world of online dating were beyond positive. But they were not 100% positive. Yes, the highs outweighed the lows. Yes, the good outweighed the bad. Yes, the amusement overwhelmed the discomfort. But it only took one Elizabeth to leave a mark.

What happened with Elizabeth was not a stumble and certainly not something that couldn't or shouldn't have been avoided. The fault, however, cannot be evenly distributed. It was all mine.

I'd like to believe that I'm a better person because of my encounter with Elizabeth. But I know it would have been preferable if I were a better person before.

# A final word to the wise from someone who isn't, particularly

For me, the cyberspace dating episodes were undeniably successful. The obvious reason is that I met Debbie. She is not only the icing on the cake; she's also the cake and every single candle blown out in a single breath. And, as everyone knows, if you get 'em all in one shot, all of your wishes are fulfilled.

But even before Debbie – even during the decades of failed attempts at finding her – the process was its own reward. It's undeniably true that I didn't enjoy every minute or every meeting. But my nose wouldn't grow (that would definitely be a problem because it's hardly petite now) if I claimed that I had a really good time almost all of the time.

Maybe there's a moral here. Maybe not. But I think if there is anything to be learned from my experience, it's this: the journey is just as important as the destination.

So if you're vacillating about taking the plunge into the world of internet dating, here's my advice:

Go for it.

With the right attitude, you'll definitely enjoy the trip. And with persistence and a bit of luck, like so many others have already discovered, the person you're looking for may just happen to be on the other end of the computer and looking for you.

Made in the USA
Columbia, SC
14 September 2020